# Building a Strong
# Vocabulary
## FOR WORK READINESS

Ellen Northcutt

Christine Griffith Wagner

**New Readers Press**
**ProLiteracy**'s publishing division

Building a Strong Vocabulary for Work Readiness
ISBN 978-1-56420-898-9

Copyright © 2016 New Readers Press
New Readers Press
ProLiteracy's Publishing Division
104 Marcellus Street, Syracuse, New York 13204
www.newreaderspress.com

Printed in the United States of America
10  9  8  7  6  5

Proceeds from the sale of New Readers Press materials support professional
development, training, and technical assistance programs of ProLiteracy
that benefit local literacy programs in the U.S. and around the globe.

**Editor:** Beth Oddy
**Editorial Director:** Terrie Lipke
**Designer:** Cathi Miller
**Technology Specialist:** Maryellen Casey

# CONTENTS

# TO THE LEARNER

## *Building a Strong Vocabulary for Work Readiness*

**This book will help you build the vocabulary and vocabulary skills you need to find a job and to succeed at work.**

*This is a list of the topics in the book. Do you ever talk about these things? Which of these things have you done or do you know about?*
*Check YES or NO.*

| YES | NO | |
|-----|-----|-----|
| | | Finding a job |
| | | Completing a job application |
| | | Writing a resume |
| | | Preparing for an interview |
| | | Being professional |
| | | Serving on a team |
| | | Setting and achieving goals |
| | | Understanding performance reviews |
| | | Understanding employee benefits |
| | | Understanding your paycheck |
| | | Staying safe at work |
| | | Losing a job |

As you work through this book, you will learn many ways to recognize, understand, and use words about workplace topics.

# About *Building a Strong Vocabulary for Work Readiness*

## THE UNITS

There are 12 units in this book. Each unit begins with a reading that has 12 boldfaced vocabulary words. You'll see those words throughout the unit. You'll get lots of practice defining and using them.

## VOCABULARY STRATEGIES

You'll also learn vocabulary strategies you can use to build your vocabulary. These strategies will improve your reading and writing skills as well. And that will help you at home, in your community, at work, and at school.

### Word Parts

You will learn about breaking words into parts, including prefixes, suffixes, and roots. When you know the meanings of word parts, you can often figure out a word's meaning. You will also learn many compound words and how to figure out their meanings.

### Context

Did you know that there are clues in most readings that can help you figure out unfamiliar words? These are called context clues. You will learn how to look for different kinds of clues, such as synonyms, antonyms, examples, and definitions. You will also practice using these clues to determine the meanings of words.

### Dictionary and Parts of Speech

A dictionary is a great resource when you want to build your vocabulary. You can use a dictionary to find out how a word is pronounced, to understand what part of speech a word can play, and to learn a word's meanings. Many activities in this book will ask you to use a dictionary. The dictionary will help you to understand different parts of speech and to choose the correct meaning of a word.

### Multiple Meanings

Many words in English have more than one meaning. You will practice figuring out the correct meaning of words that you read by thinking about the context and how a word is used in a sentence.

## FEATURES

### Exercises

Practice is the best way to learn something new. So each unit has lots of activities to develop your new vocabulary and vocabulary strategies. The more you do, the more you'll learn and remember. Research shows that people learn new vocabulary when they see words several times and practice using them in different ways.

### Tips

Tips appear on the sides of many pages. You'll find helpful hints there. Some tips give information about specific words, such as how to say or spell them. Others describe strategies that you can use to figure out word meanings. Read the tips before you do the exercises. They can help you complete the exercises and develop your vocabulary skills.

### Personalization Activities

Many pages include questions for you to answer using your own experiences, ideas, and knowledge. There are no right or wrong answers to these activities. Asking and answering personal questions is an excellent way to practice and remember new words. You will be able to practice your writing, speaking, and listening skills as you complete these activities.

### Answer Key and Word Part Lists

You can check your answers by looking in the Answer Key at the back of the book. You will also find lists of common prefixes, suffixes, and roots there. These lists will be good resources even after you finish the book.

### Personal Dictionary

Use the Personal Dictionary on page 112 to keep track of new words you learn.

## SETTING GOALS

Many students define their success in school by setting and meeting goals. A goal is something you want to achieve. You may have a goal for using this book. Maybe you want to be a better reader. Maybe you want to get a better job. Maybe you want to pass a test.

Complete this sentence:

I'm using this book because I want to _____

_____

Come back and review this page every few weeks. You may find that you need or want to revise your goal.

# 1 Finding a Job

## VOCABULARY

Read these words from the passage. Check the words you know.

- ☐ apply
- ☐ benefits
- ☐ employer
- ☐ employment
- ☐ hire
- ☐ job fair
- ☐ keyword
- ☐ network
- ☐ salary
- ☐ skills
- ☐ temporary
- ☐ training

### Abbreviations

FT (full-time)

PT (part-time)

**Looking for a job can be stressful. To be successful in a job search, understand different kinds of jobs and how to find them.**

You will need to spend time and energy to find a job. That is why you should treat a job search like full-time work. Before you look for a job, think about your **skills** and the different kinds of work you can do.

### Types of Work

There are different types of **employment**. Many full-time jobs have a 40-hour workweek. Full-time jobs often come with **benefits** such as health insurance and paid vacation. Some full-time workers earn an annual **salary**, while others are paid by the hour.

Part-time jobs vary from a few hours to 30 or more hours a week. Most part-time jobs pay workers hourly and do not provide benefits. A **temporary** job lasts for a set period of time, such as the summer months or the holiday season.

### Looking for a Job

How do you find job openings? Start by **networking**, or talking to friends, family, neighbors, and people you worked for in the past. They may know of open positions. You should also visit the nearest workforce center. In most states, these state offices have lists of jobs. They also offer free help to job hunters, such as job **training**, resume reviews, and interview tips. **Job fairs** are another place to learn of jobs. These events provide a place for **employers** and job hunters to meet.

You can also search for a job on the Internet. Employment websites list many kinds of jobs. On these sites, you enter **keywords** about the kind of position you are looking for, such as "sales" or "restaurant." The site will show available job listings. Some company websites list their open positions. You may even be able to **apply** online.

No matter how you look for a job, it is important to talk to the people who **hire**. Don't give up if you don't find a job right away. Finding a job can take a lot of work, but the effort is worth it.

*What other words about finding a job do you know? Write them here.*

_____  _____  _____

# 1. Vocabulary Focus

*Write each word from the list beside its definition.*

| apply | benefits | employer | employment | hire | job fair |
|-------|----------|----------|------------|------|----------|
| keyword | network | salary | skills | temporary | training |

_____ 1. an event where companies can meet with people looking for jobs

_____ 2. the process of learning skills you need for a job

_____ 3. a word that you use to search for information on a computer

_____ 4. to connect and talk with other people about work or finding jobs

_____ 5. extra things you get from your employer on top of your pay, such as insurance or paid time off

_____ 6. to employ or give a job to someone

_____ 7. work that is done for money

_____ 8. money that a worker gets paid for doing a job

_____ 9. lasting for a limited or short period of time

_____ 10. to ask in writing for a job

_____ 11. the things you know how to do well

_____ 12. a person or company that pays people to work

# 2. Use the Vocabulary

*Write about some of the things you can do to find a job. Use at least three words from the vocabulary list. Circle the words you use.*

_____

_____

_____

_____

_____

_____

## 3. Work With New Vocabulary

*Write your answers to the questions. Then compare answers with a partner.*

1. Describe your **skills**.

   _____

2. Describe a good **employer** and a bad **employer**.

   _____

When people talk about temporary work or workers, they sometimes use the shortened adjective *temp* or the noun *temps*:

*The temp agency has lots of office jobs.*

*Before Christmas, the store hires a lot of temps.*

3. Would you rather have a **temporary** job or a full-time job? Explain your choice.

   _____

4. How can **networking** help a person who is looking for a job?

   _____

5. If you went to a **job fair**, how would you dress and act? Explain why.

   _____

6. How can **training** help someone get a job?

   _____

7. Paid holidays, health insurance, and sick days are some examples of **benefits**. Which benefit is most important to you? Why?

   _____

8. Who should make a larger **salary**, the U.S. president or a star basketball player? Why?

   _____

9. If you were looking for a new job, what **keywords** would you use for an online job search?

   _____

10. If you had to **hire** workers, what would you look for?

   _____

11. Do you think it is easy or hard to find **employment** where you live? Explain why.

   _____

12. Would you rather **apply** for a job online or in person? Explain your answer.

   _____

## 4. Root *pos*

**The root *pos* means "place" or "put." Read definitions of some words that are built on the root *pos*:**

**position:** a job or place in a company
**deposit:** to put money in a bank
**post:** a place where someone does a job
**posture:** the way you hold or place your body
**compose:** to write down ideas
**proposal:** a plan that is put in writing

A **root** is a word part that can be combined with other roots, prefixes, or suffixes to form a word. Many English words have roots that come from Latin and Greek. You can often use what you know about roots to figure out a word's meaning.

*Complete each sentence with one of the words from the list above.*

1. Jerome will _____ his paycheck in the bank.

2. The workforce center helped Maria _____ her resume.

3. When you meet an employer, have good _____. Don't slouch!

4. The soldier was told to stay at her _____. She was not supposed to walk around.

5. The restaurant has an open _____ for a cook.

6. The company wrote a _____ for a new office building.

## 5. Suffix *–ful*

**A suffix is a word part at the end of a word. The suffix *–ful* means "full of." You can add *–ful* to the end of some nouns to make adjectives. For example, the noun *fear* + the suffix *–ful* = the adjective *fearful*.**

*Complete each sentence with a word from the list. Check a dictionary if you don't know the meaning of a word.*

| careful | hopeful | stressful | successful |
|---------|---------|-----------|------------|

The suffix *–ful* is spelled with only one *l*.

1. Kara is _____ that she will find a job soon.

2. To be _____ at finding a job, you have to spend time and energy.

3. Alberto thought the job was very _____. He had to do a lot of work in a very short time.

4. Be _____ when you apply for a job. Make sure all your information is correct.

*Add the suffix –ful to these words. Then use each word in a sentence.*

5. thought _____

6. help _____

## 6. Compound Words

A compound is made up of two or more other words. A compound can be written as one word (*keyword*), as two words (*job fair*), or with hyphens between words (full-time). You can usually figure out the meaning of a compound by thinking about the meaning of each shorter word in the compound.

*Write a compound word from the list to match each clue.*

| full-time | job board | part-time | workforce | workweek |
|-----------|-----------|-----------|-----------|----------|

_____  1. all the people in an area who can work

_____  2. the hours in a week that people usually work

_____  3. for the full number of hours in a week that people work or go to school

_____  4. for some of the hours that people work or go to school

_____  5. a place, such as a wall or a website, where available jobs are listed

## 7. Context Clues: Synonyms

Sometimes you can look for clue words that show an author is using a synonym. The words *also, like, same,* and *too* can sometimes signal synonyms.

You can often figure out the meaning of a word by looking at the context, or the words that come before and after it. You may be able to find a synonym, or a word that means almost the same as an unfamiliar word. For example, in this sentence, *wages* and *pay* mean about the same thing:

*Juan was unhappy with his wages, and Pablo thought his pay was low, too.*

*Read each sentence. Look for context clues to help you figure out the meaning of the boldfaced word. Circle the word or words that are a synonym for the boldfaced word.*

1. Eva has a job, but she is **seeking** a new one. She is looking for a job with better pay.

2. Eva **earns** $12 an hour at her job, but she wants to make at least $15 an hour.

3. She also wants more **opportunities** at work. For example, she wants the chance to be a team leader.

4. Eva read about an interesting **position** online. The job was at a large store.

5. The store offered Eva a job, but the **compensation** was low. Eva wants a job with better pay.

6. The company **provides** workers with health insurance that costs a lot. It also gives workers only a few paid days off each year.

# 8. Parts of Speech and the Dictionary

**Some words can be used for more than one part of speech. For example, *search* can be both a noun ("the act of looking for something") and a verb ("to look for"). Before you look up a word in the dictionary, identify its part of speech. To figure this out, look at how the word is used in the sentence.**

*Look up each boldfaced word in a dictionary. Write the part of speech and the definition that matches how the word is used in the sentence.*

1. A job **hunt** can take weeks, months, or even longer.

_____  _____

2. Find out how long a temporary job will **last** before you agree to take it.

_____  _____

3. You should **treat** a job search like it's your full-time job.

_____  _____

4. The woman at the job center was very **kind**. She helped Kay apply for jobs.

_____  _____

5. Many stores hire workers for the holiday **season**.

_____  _____

> If you read a word that you don't know, think about how the word works in the sentence. What part of speech does it play—noun, verb, adverb, or adjective? Knowing the part of speech can be one clue to a word's meaning.

# 9. Multiple-Meaning Words

**Some words have more than one meaning. To figure out the correct meaning, look at how the word is used in the sentence. You can also look at nearby words for clues.**

*Look at each underlined word. Circle the letter of the best definition.*

1. Lee works for a small <u>company</u>. There are only 10 employees.
   a. guests
   b. business

2. The website lists <u>current</u> job openings.
   a. the movement of water
   b. happening now

3. Look for a job that will <u>interest</u> you.
   a. to hold your attention
   b. extra money that a bank pays you for keeping money there

4. Make a <u>plan</u> for how you will find a job.
   a. a set of things to do
   b. a map of a building

5. Your job should <u>match</u> your skills and interests.
   a. a sports event between players or teams
   b. to work together with or be suitable

*Read the paragraph. Circle the word or words that best complete each sentence.*

Lily needs to a find a job. She has been looking for a month. But so far, she has not been (1) *successful / thoughtful*. Lily went to some hotels and restaurants and asked about jobs. She also went to a (2) *network / job fair*, but there were a lot of other people looking for jobs there. Lily knew that she needed a (3) *plan / posture* for how to (4) *last / hunt* for a job. She decided to go to the (5) *workforce / benefits* center. Lily was (6) *careful / hopeful* that the center could help.

*Complete the brochure. Use words from the list.*

| apply | employers | job board | match | provide | seeking | skills | stressful | training |

## Welcome to the Job and Career Center!

We know that looking for a job can be difficult and (7) _____. But we are here to (8) _____ help to people who are (9) _____ jobs.

### Here are a few ways we can help you if you are looking for work:

We can help you figure out what (10) _____ you have and what you do well. Then we use that information to help (11) _____ you to the right kinds of jobs.

- We offer classes and (12) _____ in areas like computers and office work. We can help you learn what you need to know.

- We can help you (13) _____ for jobs. This includes help with your resume or job application.

- We have an online (14) _____. It lists jobs from (15) _____ in our area.

*Read each question. Then circle the best answer.*

1. **What does the word *deposits* mean in this sentence?**

   At the end of each day, Chen <u>deposits</u> all the money from the shop in the bank.

   **A** earns

   **B** places

   **C** spends

   **D** works

2. **Which word describes a person who offers a lot of help?**

   **A** helpful

   **B** helpless

   **C** unhelpful

   **D** helplessly

3. **Which definition of *network* matches how the word is used in this sentence?**

   You can <u>network</u> online or in person to find out about jobs.

   **A** to connect computers together

   **B** a group of computers that are linked together

   **C** a group of TV stations that are connected

   **D** to meet and talk with others about work

4. **Which word best completes the passage?**

   The store has two open _____ for salespeople. You can apply online.

   **A** employers

   **B** positions

   **C** benefits

   **D** job fairs

5. **Which word best completes the sentence?**

   Frank works Tuesday through Saturday and has a 40-hour _____.

   **A** worker

   **B** workforce

   **C** network

   **D** workweek

6. **Which words from the passage mean about the same as *salary*?**

   Bob's monthly pay at his new job is about $3,000. His <u>salary</u> at his old job was $2,500 per month. Bob is saving the extra money to buy a house.

   **A** monthly pay

   **B** new job

   **C** per month

   **D** buy a house

7. **Kim wants to get a job for just three months this summer. Which choice best describes the kind of job she is looking for?**

   **A** full-time

   **B** part-time

   **C** temporary

   **D** training

8. **What does the word *company* mean in this sentence?**

   Darlene works for a <u>company</u> that makes cell phones and computers.

   **A** guests in your home

   **B** friends or people you spend time with

   **C** a business that makes or sells things

   **D** a group of actors or dancers

*If you wanted to find a job, what would you do? Write your answer on a separate piece of paper. Use at least six words you learned in this unit. Circle the vocabulary words you used.*

*Check your answers on page 104.*

# 2 Completing a Job Application

## VOCABULARY

- [ ] accurate
- [ ] applicable
- [ ] chronological
- [ ] contact information
- [ ] detailed
- [ ] process
- [ ] professional
- [ ] proofread
- [ ] references
- [ ] sample
- [ ] submit
- [ ] value

### Abbreviations

DOB (date of birth)

N/A (not applicable)

SSN (Social Security number)

**For many job hunters, filling out a job application is the first step in getting a job. For many employers, a job application is their first introduction to a future employee. A job application shows an employer what you've done and what you can do.**

You need a lot of information to complete a job application successfully. To make the **process** easier, you can review and complete **sample** job applications on paper or online. Do an online search on the phrase "sample job application forms." You will find sample applications at many websites. Pick one and complete it. There are job centers in every state that will review your sample for free. Or you can ask someone whose opinion you **value** to look over your application. Keep your completed sample job application with you, and use it as a guide when you complete a real application.

Every application is a little different, but you usually start with your personal **contact information**. You also need a **detailed** employment history in which you list your most recent employment first, and move back in **chronological** order. You need the same information for your education.

Most employers ask for **references**. Prepare a list of references before applying for a job. These should be people who can answer questions about your skills and qualifications. References can be **professional** or personal. Pick your references carefully and be sure each one agrees to act as a reference for you before you list him or her. You don't want someone to be surprised when a possible employer calls to ask about you!

Read through each application form completely before filling it out. Complete the application in blue or black ink. Always **proofread** your application. Thoroughly reread it to make sure there are no spelling or grammar errors and all the information is **accurate**. Don't leave anything blank. If a question does not apply to you, write N/A (not **applicable**.)

Sign and date the form before you **submit** it. When you sign a job application, you are saying that everything you have written is true and correct. If it isn't, you might not get or keep the job.

*What other words about job applications do you know? Write them here.*

_____    _____    _____

# 1. Vocabulary Focus

*Match the word with its definition. Write the correct letter.*

_____ 1. accurate

_____ 2. applicable

_____ 3. chronological

_____ 4. contact information

_____ 5. detailed

_____ 6. process

_____ 7. professional

_____ 8. proofread

_____ 9. reference

_____ 10. sample

_____ 11. submit

_____ 12. value

a. related to a job

b. to have a high opinion of

c. a person who can recommend you for a job

d. to present an application (or other document) to somebody for review

e. your phone number, email address, street address, etc.

f. arranged in the order in which things happened

g. giving a lot of information

h. a series of actions that you take in order to achieve a result

i. relevant or appropriate

j. exactly right, with no mistakes

k. an example

l. to read and correct a piece of writing

> ● The *chr* in *chronological* is pronounced /kr/.

# 2. Use the Vocabulary

*Write about the last time you applied for something. Use at least three words from the vocabulary list. Underline the vocabulary words you use.*

_____

_____

_____

_____

_____

## 3. Work With New Vocabulary

*Answer the questions. Then compare answers with a partner.*

1. Describe a **process** you go through every day.

   _____

2. What facts are you usually asked to include when you provide your **contact information**?

   _____

3. What are some advantages of completing **sample** applications?

   _____

4. What kinds of mistakes do you look for when you **proofread** something you wrote?

   _____

5. What are some things you do at school, at work, or at home that require you to be **accurate**? Why is it important to do those things accurately?

   _____

6. Describe what you did today in **chronological** order.

   _____

7. What forms did you have to **submit** when you started school?

   _____

8. Why do you think it is important to write "not **applicable**" on a job application next to questions that don't apply to you?

   _____

9. What would you hope a **professional** reference would write about you in a letter of reference?

   _____

10. Name someone or something that you **value**. Explain your answer.

    _____

11. What information do you need to include in a **detailed** job or education history?

    _____

12. If you were applying for a job, what two people would you ask to be your **references**? Explain your choices.

    _____

## 4. Prefix re–

**When the prefix re– is placed before a root word, it means "again" and "back."**

*Read each word and its definition. Then use the word in a sentence.*

1. **reconsider:** to rethink a decision or opinion

   _____

2. **recall:** to bring the memory of a past event into your mind

   _____

3. **rearrange:** to change the order, position, or time of arrangements already made

   _____

Watch out for words with letter groups that look like prefixes, but aren't, for example *recent*.

*Use a word from the list to complete each sentence. Check a dictionary if you don't know the meaning of a word.*

| recall | reread | return |
|--------|--------|--------|

4. Julia is going to pick up the application at the store on Monday, complete it at home, and

   _____ it to the store on Tuesday.

5. After you finish a job application, _____ it carefully. Proofread it for all spelling and grammar mistakes.

6. Rudi couldn't _____ the address or phone number of her previous jobs, and she didn't have the information with her. She asked if she could take the application home to complete it.

## 5. Suffixes –ation, –cation, –ion, –tion

**The suffixes –ation, –cation, –ion, and –tion mean "the act or process of." Words that end in –ation, –cation, –ion, and –tion are nouns.**

*Use a word from the list to complete each sentence. Check a dictionary if you don't know the meaning of a word.*

| application | discussion | position | qualifications |
|-------------|------------|----------|----------------|

1. Jasmine applied for a part-time _____ working in the school library.

2. Joe included his knowledge of different computer languages and his strong communication skills among his _____ for the programmer's job.

3. Did you complete the _____ online or in person?

4. Miguel had a long _____ with his family about which jobs he should apply for.

# 6. Compound Words

**If you don't know the meaning of a compound word, think about what each word part means.**

*Complete the sentences. Use words from the list.*

| double check | feedback | guidelines | websites | workforce center |
| --- | --- | --- | --- | --- |

1. There's a _____ on the east side of town where counselors will help you with your job hunt, and it's free.

2. Most large companies list jobs on their _____, so my career counselor recommended I look for work online.

3. Always _____ your completed job application before you hand it in.

4. Share your completed sample application with others and ask them for _____ on ways to improve it.

5. Follow these _____ for completing a job application.

# 7. Context Clues: Definitions and General Context

**Look for hints and clues to figure out words you don't know.**

*Underline words that help explain each boldfaced word. Then write a definition.*

1. If you do a careful job completing your application, you show a **potential** employer that you will be a careful worker.

   _____

2. You will need to provide information about any **former** employers. Companies usually contact people you worked for in the past.

   _____

3. There are often hundreds of **candidates** for every job opening. Make sure your application helps you stand out from the other people applying for the job.

   _____

4. If an application asks about your activities or interests, include things that seem **relevant**. Don't just list things you like to do; list only things that are connected to the job.

   _____

5. Make sure you fill out your application **legibly**. It's important to write clearly and neatly.

   _____

6. When you sign a job application, you **verify** that what you wrote is true and accurate.

   _____

# 8. Parts of Speech and the Dictionary

**To figure out the meaning of a word, look at how it is used in the sentence. A verb names an action or describes a state of being. A noun names a person, place, thing, or idea.**

*Look up each boldfaced word in a dictionary. Write the part of speech and the definition that matches how the word is used in the sentence.*

1. **Tailor** your answers to the job you are applying for. Show why you are qualified for this particular job.

   _____  _____

2. If an employer can't read your writing, it could **cost** you the job.

   _____  _____

3. Many employers **screen** applications. They leave out forms that are not complete, signed, or clean.

   _____  _____

4. Remember to **contact** your references before you share their information on a job application.

   _____  _____

5. Completing a job application is the first **step** in the hiring process.

   _____  _____

# 9. Multiple-Meaning Words

**Many words can have more than one meaning. To figure out the correct meaning, look at nearby words for clues.**

*Look at each underlined word. Circle the letter of the best definition.*

1. When you describe past jobs and work experience, <u>highlight</u> your skills and abilities.
   a. to emphasize
   b. to mark something, such as text, with a bright color

2. Carry a completed <u>model</u> application with you.
   a. a small copy of something
   b. a good example of something

3. <u>Note</u> your education, whether it is a college education, high school diploma, or HSE.
   a. to notice and remember something
   b. to write something down

4. Include your <u>dates</u> of employment in your work history.
   a. time periods
   b. agreements to meet someone at a particular time or on a particular day

5. Don't leave any <u>blanks</u> on your job application.
   a. empty spaces in a line of writing or on a form
   b. events or a time that cannot be remembered

*Complete the guidelines. Use words from the list.*

| accurate | applicable | blanks | chronological | contact information | guidelines |
|---|---|---|---|---|---|
| legibly | references | proofread | sample | screen | steps | submit |

# Tips for Completing a Winning Job Application

**The Workforce Center**
**86 Hayward Avenue**
**TWC@NRP**

- One of the most important (1) _____ in getting a job is filling out the application form. Here are some (2) _____ to help you do the best job possible!

- Be prepared. Always carry a copy of your completed (3) _____ application with you.

- Also take a list of people who have agreed to be your (4) _____. Make sure their (5) _____ is up to date and (6) _____.

- List your education and job history in reverse (7) _____ order.

- Write (8) _____. Many companies (9) _____ applications for neatness as well as errors.

- Don't leave any (10) _____ on the application. If necessary, write N/A, or not (11) _____.

- Don't (12) _____ your application until you (13) _____ it at least two times.

*Good luck!*

*Read each question. Then circle the best answer.*

1.  **Which definition of *values* matches the meaning in this passage?**

    Andy asked his former boss and two coworkers to be his references. He asked them because he <u>values</u> their opinion.

    **A** to estimate the worth of

    **B** to think highly of

    **C** to love

    **D** to evaluate

2.  **Which of these words means "remember"?**

    **A** rethink

    **B** reconsider

    **C** remind

    **D** recall

3.  **Which definition of *contact* matches the meaning in this passage?**

    Don't leave any blanks on your application. If you don't have a phone, provide the number of someone who can easily <u>contact</u> you.

    **A** to touch or hit someone

    **B** a person you know who can help you

    **C** to communicate with someone or something

    **D** to write to someone or something

4.  **What does the word *model* mean in this sentence?**

    Jill used her <u>model</u> application form to help her complete the actual one she found on the company's website.

    **A** a person who displays clothes

    **B** a person or thing that is a good example to copy

    **C** a small copy of something

    **D** one of the cars, machines, etc. that a company makes

5.  **What does the word *detailed* mean in these directions from a job application?**

    "Provide a <u>detailed</u> description of your responsibilities at each job."

    **A** highly decorated

    **B** including a lot of information

    **C** clean

    **D** complicated

6.  **Which definition of *cost* matches the meaning in this passage?**

    How important is it for all of the information on your job application to be correct? If there are errors, it could <u>cost</u> you the job . . . now or later.

    **A** to require someone to suffer

    **B** to have a price of

    **C** to cause someone to pay an amount of money

    **D** to make someone lose something

7.  **Which of these choices is closest in meaning to "to proofread?"**

    **A** to review

    **B** to lip read

    **C** to research

    **D** to misread

8.  **Which word best completes the sentence?**

    On his application, Wayne wrote the _____ he started and ended his last two jobs.

    **A** dates

    **B** processes

    **C** blanks

    **D** notes

*What advice would you give to a friend who is applying for a job for the first time? Write your answer on a separate sheet of paper. Use at least six words you learned in this unit. Circle the vocabulary words you use.*

*Check your answers on page 104.*

# 3 Writing a Resume

## VOCABULARY

Read these words from the passage. Check the words you know.

- [ ] accomplishments
- [ ] awards
- [ ] cover letter
- [ ] customize
- [ ] document
- [ ] feature
- [ ] keywords
- [ ] software
- [ ] relevant
- [ ] resume
- [ ] specific
- [ ] template

**In addition to filling out job applications, job hunters are often asked to submit resumes. What would you need to know and do in order to write your own resume today?**

A **resume** is usually a one-page **document** including your contact information, work history, education background, and personal skills. Employers are more likely to read a neat and well-written resume. You may be perfect for a job, but hiring managers will never know that if they won't even look at your resume.

Experts suggest that you start with a resume **template** and that you **customize** it for each job you apply for. One way to personalize your resume is to include **keywords**, words or terms that are **relevant** to the job. You can identify the **specific** keywords you should use by reading three or more descriptions for the kind of job you're interested it and seeing which words are used most often. Because your resume may be read by **software** that looks for keywords, using the right words increases the chance that your resume will get attention.

Your resume should be more than just a list of your past job responsibilities. Use action verbs that **feature** your key **accomplishments**. Focus on how your skills and successes contributed to the success of your team or department. Include any **awards** you've been given. Show how you have been a strong leader and communicator. Give examples.

Check your resume for spelling errors and grammar mistakes. Use spell-check and then reread the document yourself. Ask a friend to look at it as well. If you're applying for a job online, send yourself a practice email with your resume attached. Make sure you're sending the right document and that it opens correctly.

Include a **cover letter** with your resume. Your cover letter is the first thing employers see when they open your application materials. A cover letter is informative and allows you to address qualifications that you didn't include in your resume. Keep the specific employer's needs and the job requirements in mind as you write.

*What other words about resumes and cover letters do you know? Write them here.*

_____  _____  _____

# 1. Vocabulary Focus

*Match each word with its definition. Write the correct letter.*

_____ 1. accomplishments

_____ 2. award

_____ 3. cover letter

_____ 4. customize

_____ 5. keyword

_____ 6. feature

_____ 7. document

_____ 8. relevant

_____ 9. resume

_____ 10. software

_____ 11. specific

_____ 12. template

a.  a written list of your education and work experience that you use when you are looking for work

b.  to change something to make it fit the needs of a specific person or business

c.  to give special attention to something important

d.  a computer document that has the basic format of something and can be used many times

e.  an official paper with important information

f.  particular; exact and clear

g.  achievements

h.  a letter that gives more information about another document

i.  something that is given to someone for doing something well

j.  a word that is used to find information in a piece of writing, in a computer document, or on the Internet

k.  programs that run on computers

l.  connected with what you are talking or writing about

● *Keyword* can be written as one or two words.

● *Resume* can also be spelled *résumé* or *resumé*.

# 2. Use the Vocabulary

*Give a friend advice about writing a resume. Use at least three words from the vocabulary list. Underline the vocabulary words in your writing.*

_____

_____

_____

_____

_____

# 3. Work With New Vocabulary

*Answer the questions. Then compare answers with a partner.*

1. You can use a **template** to write your resume. What other documents or objects can you create using a template?

   _____

2. What is your proudest personal **accomplishment**? Explain your answer.

   _____

3. What information would you **feature** on your resume?

   _____

4. What is a **specific** piece of information that you shouldn't include on your resume or cover letter? Why not?

   _____

5. What is the first thing you think hiring managers look at on a **resume**? Explain your answer.

   _____

6. What is something you've **customized** for yourself or a friend or family member? What did you do to make it personal?

   _____

7. How would you determine if your work skills and experiences are **relevant** to a job you're applying for?

   _____

8. What are four **keywords** you would include in your search for the perfect job?

   _____

9. Name something about yourself that you would include in a **cover letter**, but not in your resume. Explain your answer.

   _____

10. What is an **award** that you've won or would like to win? What did you do or what would you have to do to earn that award?

    _____

11. Where do you keep important **documents**?

    _____

12. How have you used computer **software** at work or at home?

    _____

# 4. Prefixes *in-*, *im-*

**The prefixes *in-* and *im-* mean "in" or "into." Use *im-* with base words that begin with *b*, *m*, and *p*.**

*Complete each sentence with a word from the list.*

| impression | improve | include | increases |
|---|---|---|---|

1. Your cover letter is the first thing employers see when they open your application materials. It needs to make a positive _____ .

2. Remember to _____ active words that feature your qualifications and the job requirements.

3. Melanie used her cover letter to highlight how she helped _____ sales in the coat department at her last job.

4. A good resume _____ your chances of getting an interview.

*The underlined words below have been defined for you. Use each word in a sentence.*

5. <u>imply</u>: to suggest something without actually saying it

_____

6. <u>infer</u>: to use the information you have to decide if something is true

_____

# 5. Suffixes *-ive*, *-ative*, *-itive*

**The suffixes *-ive*, *-ative*, and *-itive* can help form adjectives from verbs. For example, someone who is *competitive* likes to compete.**

*Write a definition of the underlined word in each sentence. Use a dictionary to check your answers.*

1. If possible, include both your phone number and email address. Doing this gives employers an <u>alternative</u>, or other possible way, to reach you.

   definition: _____

2. Make sure your resume is <u>informative</u> and tells the reader about you and what you can do.

   definition: _____

3. There's no point in being <u>deceptive</u>. Most employers will do a background check and will find out if you haven't told the truth.

   definition: _____

4. Your resume and cover letter should not be <u>repetitive</u>. Each one should be original and unique.

   definition: _____

# 6. Compound Words

**Think about the meanings of the parts of a compound word.**

*Complete each sentence. Use a word from the list.*

| brainstorm | job opening | people skills |
|---|---|---|
| showcase | spell-check | summary statement |

1. A well-written resume will _____ your skills in the best possible way.

2. Tia included a _____ at the top of her resume. She wrote a short description of her job experiences that were most like the job she was applying for.

3. There's a _____ for a receptionist at the newspaper. Do you know if Melissa is going to apply?

4. People with effective _____ easily get along with their coworkers.

5. One way to avoid mistakes on your resume is to run a _____ on your computer. It's usually included in the word-processing program.

6. Before you write your resume, sit down with a friend or family member and _____ a list of as many of your skills as you can.

# 7. Context Clues: Definitions, Synonyms, and Antonyms

A thesaurus is a printed or online reference of synonyms and sometimes of antonyms.

**Your knowledge of synonyms (words that have the same or similar meanings) and antonyms (words that have opposite meanings) can help you determine the meaning of an unknown word.**

*Underline examples that help explain each boldfaced word. Then write a definition for the word.*

1. Hiring managers **appreciate** receiving customized resumes. They recognize and value the fact that you understand what they are looking for.

   definition: _____

2. Nate didn't write a chronological resume based on his work history; he wrote a **functional** resume that focused on his skills and experience.

   definition: _____

3. A resume should **emphasize**, not downplay or understate, things that are special about you.

   definition: _____

4. Bella's resume was simple, uncomplicated, and **straightforward**.

   definition: _____

5. Carter's cover letter was **concise**—short and to the point, but still interesting and complete.

   definition: _____

# 8. Parts of Speech and the Dictionary

**You can't stop reading just because you come across a word you don't know. One thing you can do is to think about what part of speech the unknown word plays.**

*Write the part of speech of the boldfaced word in each sentence. Check a dictionary if you aren't sure.*

● Remember that if a word names something, it's a noun. If it tells an action, it's a verb.

_____   1.  Sabrina made a **list** of her professional qualifications.

_____   2.  You should **list** your job experience in backwards chronological order.

_____   3.  **Research** shows that most employers won't read a resume with grammar mistakes or typos.

_____   4.  **Research** the company you are applying to, and include relevant information in your cover letter.

_____   5.  James read the job **notice** online and sent out his resume right away.

_____   6.  Unfortunately, he didn't **notice** that the job required skills he didn't have.

# 9. Multiple-Meaning Words

**Some words that are spelled the same have different meanings. Sometimes they also have different pronunciations.**

*Look at each underlined word. Circle the letter of the best definition.*

1.  Write your resume so that the hiring manager sees immediately that you <u>add</u> value to the company.
    a.  find the sum of
    b.  cause something to have

2.  Your resume should <u>look</u> professional.
    a.  appear
    b.  direct your eyes in a specific direction

3.  If you don't know the name of the person you're writing to, <u>address</u> your cover letter to "Dear Hiring Manager."
    a.  write on an envelope or package the name and address of the person you are sending it to
    b.  the name and address of the person you are sending a package or letter to

● As a noun, *address* can be pronounced uh-DRESS or ADD-dress. As a verb, it is pronounced uh-DRESS.

4.  In your cover letter, <u>reference</u> the job you're applying for.
    a.  a person who can answer questions about your skills and qualifications
    b.  mention someone or something

5.  End your cover letter with a way for the hiring manager to <u>reach</u> you.
    a.  arrive somewhere
    b.  be able to contact someone

# Unit 3 Review

*Complete the paragraphs. Use words from the lists.*

| accomplishments | emphasized | job opening | keywords | research | summary statement | team player |
|---|---|---|---|---|---|---|

Because Jenna and her family moved from Portland to Boston, she needed to look for a new job. She did some

(1) _____ online and found a (2) _____ for a school nurse that

interested her.

Jenna started her resume with a (3) _____ in which she spoke about her

(4) _____ as a nurse's aide at a school in Portland. The rest of her resume

(5) _____ her skills and experience. She used (6) _____ from the ad,

and she mentioned the award she had won for being a (7) _____.

| brainstorm | cover letter | documents | include | informative | specific | spell-check |
|---|---|---|---|---|---|---|

When Jenna finished her resume, she ran a (8) _____ to find any mistakes

in spelling or grammar. She also asked her husband to review the content. Then, Jenna wrote her

(9) _____. She asked her husband to help her (10) _____ ideas about

what (11) _____ information she should (12) _____. It took her a long

time, but when she was done, Jenna was satisfied that both (13) _____ were well written and

(14) _____.

*Read each question. Then circle the best answer.*

1. **Which definition of *potential* matches the meaning in this sentence?**

   If you don't have a lot of work experience, your resume should emphasize your <u>potential</u>.

   A  capable of becoming real
   B  qualities that exist and can be developed
   C  possible, not actual
   D  likely to happen

2. **Which word best completes the passage?**

   Employers receive hundreds of resumes and cover letters for every job opening. They appreciate getting a _____ and easy-to-read document.

   A  concise
   B  repetitive
   C  deceptive
   D  prospective

3. **Choose the best answer to this question.**

   Which of the following should Jordan <u>customize</u> in her cover letter?

   A  her spell-check
   B  her email
   C  her summary statement
   D  her address

4. **Which word correctly completes the sentence?**

   Your resume should be _____ to the job you're applying for.

   A  relevant
   B  functional
   C  straightforward
   D  attractive

5. **Which word best completes the passage?**

   Matt's counselor told him to customize his cover letter. She said it would _____ the possibility that the hiring manager would look at his resume.

   A  impress
   B  include
   C  imply
   D  increase

6. **What does the word *features* mean in this sentence?**

   Kim's resume <u>features</u> her volunteer work as well as her paid work experience.

   A  parts of the face
   B  gives special attention to
   C  imagines
   D  interesting or important parts

7. **Which word correctly completes the sentence?**

   Ty's new job pays well, but the work is a little _____.

   A  repeated
   B  repeatedly
   C  repetition
   D  repetitive

8. **Which word best completes the passage?**

   Justin worked at Harmon Industries for six years. During that time, he won four _____ for leadership and teamwork.

   A  documents
   B  accomplishments
   C  references
   D  awards

*What process would you follow if you had to write a resume for the job of your dreams? Write your answer on a separate piece of paper. Use at least six words you learned in this unit. Circle the vocabulary words you use.*

*Check your answers beginning on page 104.*

# 4 Preparing for an Interview

## VOCABULARY

Read these words from the passage. Check the words you know.

- ☐ appropriately
- ☐ candidate
- ☐ common
- ☐ contribute
- ☐ convince
- ☐ decision
- ☐ impression
- ☐ interview
- ☐ offer
- ☐ prepare
- ☐ screen
- ☐ valuable

**A job interview is an important step in finding a job. Read about the interview process.**

Most companies get many resumes and applications for job openings. They have to **screen** many applicants and decide who would be best for their company. Getting a job **interview** is a positive step toward getting a job. It is a chance for you to **convince** the company to hire you.

### Before the Interview

Making a good **impression** is important at an interview. That is why you must **prepare**. Good preparation can be the difference between getting an **offer** and missing out on a job.

Research the job and the company. Read the job description carefully to understand the job requirements and job duties. Think about how your skills and experience would be useful. Learn about the company and make sure you know the products or services they offer.

Prepare answers to **common** interview questions. Hiring managers often ask about a **candidate's** strengths and weaknesses. They also ask why someone wants the job or is leaving a current job. Think about your answers ahead of time.

### At the Interview

Arrive a few minutes early for your interview. Dress neatly and **appropriately**. This means no jeans or T-shirts, even if the office is casual. Bring extra copies of your resume as well as paper and a pen for taking notes. Shake hands with the people you meet. Smile and make eye contact with the people you talk to.

An interview is not a job offer. You must show the employer how you would be **valuable** to the company. Show interest by asking questions about the position and the company, but don't ask about pay or benefits until you get an offer.

### After the Interview

Ask about next steps and when the company will make a **decision**. Take the business card of each person who interviewed you. Then follow up with a thank-you note to each of them. In your note, you can add details that show how you could **contribute** to the company.

*What other words about job interviews do you know? Write them here.*

_____  _____  _____

# 1. Vocabulary Focus

*Write each word from the list beside its definition.*

| appropriately impression | candidate interview | common offer | contribute prepare | convince screen | decision valuable |
|---|---|---|---|---|---|

_____ 1. a statement that you will give someone something, such as a job

_____ 2. to get ready to do something

_____ 3. a person who is applying for a job

_____ 4. a choice that is made after thinking about what to do

_____ 5. a feeling or opinion that you have after meeting someone

_____ 6. happening often

_____ 7. to look at people or things in order to decide if they are suitable for a particular purpose

_____ 8. in a way that is correct for a particular situation

_____ 9. to give help, ideas, or effort to something

_____ 10. useful or important

_____ 11. a meeting in which a person who wants a job is asked questions to see if he or she would be good at it

_____ 12. to make someone believe something

# 2. Use the Vocabulary

*What are some things you can do in order to have a good interview? Use at least three words from the vocabulary list. Circle the words you used.*

_____

_____

_____

_____

_____

# 3. Work With New Vocabulary

*Answer the questions. Then compare answers with a partner.*

The word *candidate* can refer to a person trying to get a job. *Candidate* can also mean a person who is trying to get elected. For example, *A year before the election, there were 15 <u>candidates</u> for president.*

1. How should a **candidate** act when meeting with an employer?

_____

2. If you want to **convince** someone that you are right, what do you do?

_____

3. When are some times that you need to make a good **impression**?

_____

4. What skills do you have that would be **valuable** to a company?

_____

5. Name some times that you should dress **appropriately**.

_____

The word *interview* can refer to different kinds of meetings in which one person asks another questions. For example, a reporter might do an *interview* of someone important for a news story, and the police might tape an *interview* with a witness or a suspect in a crime.

6. How is a job **interview** different from a job application?

_____

7. Describe some **decisions** you have made this week. Were they easy or hard decisions? Explain why.

_____

8. How do you **prepare** for a test? Why is it important to prepare?

_____

9. What are some **common** sights that you see on your way to school or work?

_____

10. Why do employers **screen** people who apply for a job?

_____

11. What would be a good job **offer** for you? Explain your answer.

_____

12. How do you **contribute** to your family, class, or job?

_____

## 4. Prefix *inter–*

The prefix *inter–* means "between" or "among." The prefix *inter–* can be added to a base word, or a word that can stand on its own: *inter + state = interstate*, meaning "between states." It can also be combined with a root: *inter + cept = intercept*, meaning "to stop something going from one place to another."

*Read each sentence. Write the meaning of the underlined word.*

1. During a job interview, listen carefully and don't <u>interrupt</u> someone who is speaking.

   interrupt: _____

2. Employers may want to know how you <u>interact</u> with others before offering you a job.

   interact: _____

3. The <u>Internet</u> can be an important tool for job hunters.

   Internet: _____

4. Jan was not sure how to <u>interpret</u> one of the questions the interviewer asked.

   interpret: _____

5. Diego had an interview at an <u>international</u> company.

   international: _____

> To figure out the meaning of a word that starts with *inter–*, try to break the word into parts. Use what you know about the prefix and the base word or root.

## 5. Roots *scrib, script*

The roots *scrib* and *script* mean "write." Read the definitions of these words with the roots *scrib* and *script*:

> **transcribe:** to write down exactly what was said
> **script:** the written form of a film or play
> **describe:** to say or write what something is like
> **subscription:** money you pay to get copies of a newspaper or magazine
> **transcript:** a written record of a student's course work and grades

*Use a word from the list above to complete each sentence.*

1. The reporter will record the interview and later _____ the speaker's words.

2. The employer asked Jane to _____ her last job and to explain why she left.

3. Hank has a _____ to the newspaper. He checks the job ads daily.

4. The college asked for a _____ of the courses Michelle took in community college.

5. The _____ for the film was 200 pages long.

> The roots *scrib* and *script* can occur at the beginning, middle, or end of a word. For example: <u>scrib</u>ble, pre<u>scrip</u>tion, de<u>scrib</u>e.

# 6. Compound Words

**To figure out the meaning of a compound word, break it into parts. Use what you know about the individual words to determine the meaning of the compound.**

*Complete each sentence with a compound word from the list.*

| business card | eye contact | handshake | hiring manager | job description |
|---|---|---|---|---|

1. Use a firm _____ with the interviewer at the beginning and end of the interview.

2. Making _____ during an interview can show that you are interested and paying attention.

3. A _____ is usually printed with a person's name, company name, job title, and contact information.

4. A _____ is responsible for interviewing and choosing a new employee.

5. The _____ tells what the successful applicant will do and the skills he or she will need.

# 7. Context Clues: Examples

The clue words *for example, such as, for instance, like,* and *including* can signal that a writer is giving examples.

**Writers sometimes give examples to help explain a word or term. Look for example clues to help you figure out the meaning of an unfamiliar term.**

*Read the paragraph. Write examples that explain each boldfaced word.*

A job counselor **coached** Tom before his job interview at a cell phone store. For example, she asked him common interview questions and helped him improve his answers. She told Tom to wear business **attire**, for instance, dress pants, a long-sleeved shirt, and a tie. They talked about the job **requirements**, which included math skills, people skills, and customer service experience. The counselor reminded Tom to learn about the store's **products**, such as cell phones, chargers, and cases. They also talked about the **duties** of the job, such as greeting customers, talking about the products, and making sales.

1. coached _____

2. attire _____

3. requirements _____

4. products _____

5. duties _____

# 8. Parts of Speech and the Dictionary

**A dictionary gives definitions of words, but it also gives information about pronunciation and parts of speech. When you look up a word, find the correct part of speech.**

*Look up each boldfaced word in a dictionary. Write the part of speech and the definition that matches how the word is used in the sentence.*

1. Tony was a **minute** late for his interview.

   _____  _____

2. Know how to **answer** common interview questions.

   _____  _____

3. Tara hopes the company will **offer** her the job within a week.

   _____  _____

4. Dylan needs more **practice** answering interview questions.

   _____  _____

5. Before your interview, learn about the company's products and **services**.

   _____  _____

> ● Sometimes a word can be pronounced in different ways. Each pronunciation can have its own meaning. For example, the word *minute* can be pronounced *MIN-it*, a noun that means 60 seconds. *Minute* can also be pronounced *my-NOOT*, an adjective that means very small.

# 9. Multiple-Meaning Words

**A word can have more than one meaning. To figure out a word's meaning, look at how it is used in the sentence.**

*Look at each underlined word. Circle the letter of the best definition.*

1. Keep a <u>positive</u> attitude when you are looking for a job.
   a. sure or certain
   b. good or useful

2. Show that you are <u>prepared</u> for the interview by learning about the company.
   a. ready
   b. made ahead of time

3. An employer may ask why you <u>left</u> your last job.
   a. the direction opposite of right
   b. stopped working for

4. A handshake should be <u>firm</u>, but not too hard.
   a. a business or company
   b. between soft and hard

5. The job <u>duties</u> include getting packages ready for shipping.
   a. tasks that are part of a job
   b. taxes you pay on items you buy in another country

> ● On a test, you may be asked to choose the best meaning of a word from several choices. Try out each answer choice in the sentence to see which one makes the most sense.

*Read the paragraph. Circle the word that best completes each sentence.*

Companies often get many resumes for a job opening, so they have to (1) *screen / describe* the applicants to find the best ones. There may be hundreds of applicants, but only a few people will get an (2) *Internet / interview*. Getting an interview is a (3) *firm / positive* step. It shows that the company is interested in you. Use the interview to make a good (4) *impression / decision* on the company.

*Carmen got this list of tips from the workforce center. Complete the sentences with words from the list.*

| answer | appropriately | attire | common | contribute |
|---|---|---|---|---|
| convince | describe | hiring manager | Internet | |
| interrupt | job description | prepare | requirements | |

## INTERVIEW TIPS

### A good interview can help you get hired. Use these tips to make sure you are ready:

- Always (5) _____ for the interview by researching the company and the people you will meet. Use the (6) _____ to find and look at the company's websites.

- Be ready for the most (7) _____ interview questions. Know how to (8) _____ these kinds of questions before your interview.

- The (9) _____ will probably ask about your current or last job. Think about the best way to (10) _____ your work. Plan to explain why you left or want to leave your job.

- Before your interview, reread the (11) _____. It will tell what the job is like and will list the (12) _____, such as the education, skills, and experience you need.

- At the interview, your task is to (13) _____ the employer that you are the best candidate for the job. Be ready to talk about how you could (14) _____ to the company.

- During the interview, listen carefully when others are speaking. Don't (15) _____.

- Dress (16) _____. Wear proper business (17) _____.

- After your interview, send a thank-you note.

*Read each question. Then circle the best answer.*

1. **Which definition of *practice* matches how the word is used in this sentence?**

   Marco needs more <u>practice</u> answering interview questions.

   **A** something people do often
   **B** the usual way of doing something
   **C** the office of a doctor or lawyer
   **D** doing an activity so you get better at it

2. **What is the meaning of *transcript* in this sentence?**

   Judy needed a copy of her GED <u>transcript</u> and diploma when she applied for a job.

   **A** a written record of a student's courses and grades
   **B** a test you take on a computer
   **C** a meeting you have with an employer before you are hired
   **D** a kind of photo identification

3. **Which of the following words means "between countries"?**

   **A** nations
   **B** nationality
   **C** international
   **D** examination

4. **Which choice best completes the passage?**

   At an interview, take the _____ of each person you meet. That way, you will have their contact information.

   **A** business card
   **B** job description
   **C** handshake
   **D** eye contact

5. **What does *valuable* mean in this passage?**

   During an interview, show how you could be a <u>valuable</u> employee. Explain how you could contribute to the company.

   **A** worth a lot of money
   **B** useful or helpful
   **C** easy to talk to
   **D** scarce or limited in amount

6. **Which choice best completes the passage?**

   William had a good interview. The next day, he received _____ and decided to take the job.

   **A** a description
   **B** an impression
   **C** a subscription
   **D** an offer

7. **Which of the following is an example of a job *duty*?**

   **A** practicing answers for interview questions
   **B** having a high school diploma
   **C** greeting customers
   **D** having two years of experience

8. **What does the word *candidates* mean in this sentence?**

   The company will interview three <u>candidates</u> before hiring one of them.

   **A** jobs that an employee will do
   **B** people who decide who will be hired
   **C** things that a company makes and sells
   **D** people applying for a job

*How should you prepare for an interview? Write your answer on a separate sheet of paper. Use at least six words you learned in this unit. Circle the vocabulary words you used.*

*Check your answers on page 105.*

# 5 Being Professional

## VOCABULARY

Read these words from the passage. Check the words you know.

- ☐ attitude
- ☐ diverse
- ☐ dress code
- ☐ expectations
- ☐ fundamental
- ☐ hobbies
- ☐ honest
- ☐ integrity
- ☐ lack
- ☐ policies
- ☐ professional
- ☐ reliable

**Every workplace and job has its own set of roles, responsibilities, and expectations. They define what it means to be professional.**

A **professional** employee is **reliable** and respectful. Although specific employability skills differ depending on your job and the work environment, it is safe to say that they will include having a good **attitude** and being open to change.

Developing these **fundamental** skills will help you get along with coworkers and make smart decisions at work. But you already do these things, even when you're not working. For example, you may have to get things done on time, understand health and safety rules, and follow a **dress code**—at school, in the community, with your **hobbies**, or when you play a sport. On the job, you will also be expected to follow company **policies**.

At work, you are part of a team that relies on you to do your job well and on time. Team players support each other. One of the best ways to do that is by acting with **integrity**. Successful work relationships are built on respect and on treating others the way you'd like to be treated. People want to be heard. If you listen carefully, you'll come to recognize the value of the **diverse** opinions, beliefs, ideas, and abilities of your supervisors, your customers, and other employees (especially if their opinions are different from your own). You'll also learn a lot and earn everyone's respect.

An important part of winning the respect of others is being **honest**. If a mistake happens, you are expected to act in a professional manner and not cover it up. If you are honest, others are likely to follow your example and be truthful with you in return. However, if you show that you **lack** integrity by lying to people about something like the number of hours you worked or why the copy machine is broken, you'll lose their trust. Employees who are not trusted are not likely to reach their goals.

On the other hand, if you make good choices and meet the **expectations** of your employers, you increase your chances of success.

*What other words do you know about being professional at work?*

_____  _____  _____

# 1. Vocabulary Focus

*Write each word from the list beside its definition.*

| attitude | diverse | dress code | expectation | fundamental | hobby |
|----------|---------|------------|-------------|-------------|-------|
| honest | integrity | lack | policies | professional | reliable |

_____  1.  honesty and sincerity

_____  2.  able to be trusted to do what is needed

_____  3.  something people like doing in their free time

_____  4.  having the skills and behaviors of a person who does his or her job well

_____  5.  a company's rules or guidelines

_____  6.  rules about what you can and cannot wear at work, at school, at a restaurant, etc.

_____  7.  to not have

_____  8.  a feeling or belief about what is expected of someone or something

_____  9.  very different from each other

_____  10.  the way you think or feel about something

_____  11.  good and truthful

_____  12.  basic; forming or relating to the most important part of something

# 2. Use the Vocabulary

*Write about a time at school, at work, or in your community when you had to deal with someone who wasn't acting like a professional. What happened? How did you feel? Use at least three words from the vocabulary list. Circle the vocabulary words you use.*

_____

_____

_____

_____

# 3. Work With New Vocabulary

*Answer the questions. Then compare answers with a partner.*

1. Why is it important to be **honest** at work?

   _____

2. Give an example of a time you showed **integrity** while getting something done at school or at work. What happened?

   _____

3. Name one of your **hobbies**. Why do you enjoy doing it?

   _____

4. What **expectations** do you have of yourself at school? At work?

   _____

5. How can you demonstrate that you have a positive **attitude**? Give two examples.

   _____

6. What are some **fundamental** skills for being good at a sport or hobby you're interested in? Explain your choices.

   _____

7. What does it mean to you to act like a **professional**?

   _____

8. What is the relationship between being a team player and respecting people from **diverse** backgrounds?

   _____

9. Describe the **dress code** you are expected to follow at work or at school.

   _____

10. Do you have a friend or coworker that you'd describe as **reliable**? What does that person do? How does that person act?

    _____

11. What are three work skills that you **lack** and would like to develop? Why are they important to you?

    _____

12. Name two **policies** you would expect employees to follow if you owned your own company. Explain your answers.

    _____

## 4. Prefix *dis-*

**The prefix *dis-* means "not" or "the opposite of." For example, *disrespect* is the opposite of *respect*.**

*Complete each sentence with a word from the list. Check a dictionary if you don't know the meaning of a word.*

| disability | disagree | dishonest | disrespect | distrust |
|---|---|---|---|---|

1. Nick and Seth _____ about where to put the new sweaters. Nick wants to put them in front of the store and Seth wants to put them in the store window.

2. It's _____ to take things like paper, pens, and tools from the office.

3. A physical _____ does not keep someone from thinking clearly, being a team player, or doing a job well.

4. At home, school, work, or play, it's never right to treat people with _____. No one should be treated wrongly or badly.

5. Your coworkers may _____ you if you often make excuses for missed due dates.

Watch out for prefix look-alikes. Some words contain the same letters as a prefix, but they are not prefixes. You know that the *dis* in *dish* is not a prefix.

When you add the prefix *dis-* to a word that begins with *s*, the new word will begin with *diss*.

## 5. Suffixes *-ity, -ty*

**The suffixes *-ity* and *-ty* can change an adjective (*able*) to a noun (*ability*). They mean "the quality of" or "the state of."**

*Complete each sentence with a word from the list. Check a dictionary if you don't know the meaning of a word.*

| difficulty | employability | equality | honesty | possibility | responsibility |
|---|---|---|---|---|---|

1. Jarvis developed his _____ skills by getting to school on time, taking part in class discussions, and helping his classmates.

2. Men and women should be treated with _____ at work. For example, women should make the same salary as men if they're doing the same work.

3. It is Carolee's _____ to turn off the lights and lock the doors at the end of the day.

4. Arthur had some _____ using the new mixer at work. It was very different from the one he had used before.

5. Mr. Stone told the department that _____ was very important to him. "As long as you tell me the truth," he said, "we can make things work."

6. Is there any _____ that you can work late tonight? We really need the extra help.

When you add the suffix *-ty* to a word that ends with *t*, the new word will end in *ty* (one *t*).

# 6. Compound Words

**Think about the meaning of the parts of a compound word when you're trying to figure out what the word means. *Dress code* is an example of a compound word used in this unit. What do you know about the two parts of *dress code*?**

*Match the compound word with its correct use.*

_____ 1. backgrounds

a. Companies often give new employees a _____ that contains important work-related information.

_____ 2. common sense

b. You can learn to be a good _____. Be an employee others know they can depend on.

_____ 3. dress code

c. Support your coworkers. Show integrity and share the _____ with others.

_____ 4. handbook

d. When you're trying to solve a problem at work, one of the best things you can do is "follow your gut" and use your _____.

_____ 5. spotlight

e. If you want to work well with people from different _____, you need to be open to new ideas.

_____ 6. team player

f. One of the first things you learn about at work is the _____. Employers want you to look professional and be safe.

# 7. Context Clues: Definitions, Examples, and General Context

**You can find context clues in the same sentence as the word you're trying to understand, or they may be in the sentence that follows.**

*Read each sentence. Look for clues to help you understand the meaning of the boldfaced word. Then write the meaning of the word.*

Note the spelling of *harassment*. It uses one *r* and a double *ss*.

1. All workplaces have a policy against **harassment**. Deliberately upsetting or bothering another employee is also against the law.

   *Harassment* means to _____

2. Dina decided to go beyond her supervisor's expectations and **exceed** her goals.

   To *exceed* means to _____

3. If you don't know the rules about how to act at work, read the section about employee **conduct** in your company handbook.

   *Conduct* means _____

4. Texting during work hours is not professional or **appropriate**. Neither is getting to work late or talking about other employees.

   *Appropriate* means _____

# 8. Parts of Speech and the Dictionary

**Some words can be used as more than one part of speech. You know what part of speech a word plays when you think about what it does in the sentence.**

*Write the part of speech of the boldfaced word in each sentence. Check a dictionary if you aren't sure.*

_____ 1. When you're at work, **focus** on your job, not on your private life.

_____ 2. If you get along with everyone, you'll get the **work** done.

_____ 3. Support and **respect** your coworkers, your supervisor, and the company.

_____ 4. **Report** to work on time.

_____ 5. Be your best at work. Get lots of **rest** the night before.

_____ 6. And try to **exercise**, too.

# 9. Multiple-Meaning Words

**Words can have different meanings depending on how they're used. Choose the definition that best fits the situation.**

*Look at each underlined word. Circle the letter of the best definition.*

Most of the commonly used words in English have multiple meanings.

1. Are you <u>open</u> to everyone's opinions?
   a. able to be entered and used by customers
   b. willing to listen to or accept different ideas

2. <u>Meet</u> and exceed your employer's expectations.
   a. to see and speak to someone for the first time
   b. to succeed in doing something

3. Gina's co-workers <u>count</u> on her to arrive and start work on time.
   a. to rely on
   b. to add together to find the total

4. If you have to <u>miss</u> work, remember to call your manager.
   a. to not be at
   b. to be late for

5. <u>Manage</u> your time by writing a to-do list and doing the most important things first.
   a. to be in control of
   b. to be in charge of a business, department, etc.

# Unit 5 Review

*Complete the guidelines below. Use words from the list.*

| attitude | diverse | expectations | professional | report | spotlight |
|----------|---------|--------------|--------------|--------|-----------|

## Guidelines for Acting Like a
### (1) _____ at Your New Job

✓ Always have a positive (2) _____. People are more likely to be friendly and helpful if they like being around you.

✓ Be open to working with people who have (3) _____ opinions, backgrounds, and beliefs. If they are different from yours, you may be surprised at what you can learn.

✓ Go out of your way to meet or go beyond your manager's (4) _____. If he or she is happy, you will be happy, too.

✓ Don't try to steal the (5) _____ from the people you work with. Everyone plays an important role in getting the job done.

✓ Show that you are reliable. (6) _____ to and leave work on time.

*Complete the paragraph. Use words from the list.*

| count | exceeds | honest | manage | responsibilities | team player |
|-------|---------|--------|--------|------------------|-------------|

Last month, Truman was named "Employee of the Year" at the tech center. His supervisor Mike said that Truman was an excellent (7) _____, and that his coworkers could (8) _____ on him to help out in any situation. Mike said that it was clear that Truman takes his (9) _____ seriously and often (10) _____ expectations.

Mike added that Truman was the most (11) _____ employee he'd ever had, and he told a funny story about one time when Truman accidentally took home two phones and drove back to work to return them.

He ended by saying how lucky he felt to be able to work with and (12) _____ Truman.

*Read each question. Then circle the best answer.*

1. **Which definition of *open* matches the meaning in this sentence?**

   Starting next week, Village Square Mall is going to open early on Saturdays.

   **A** to begin the activities of a business, school, etc.

   **B** to move a door, window, etc. so that an opening is no longer covered

   **C** to begin to use a file, document, or program on a computer

   **D** to separate the parts of something

2. **Which of these words is the opposite of *disrespect* in this passage?**

   That other manager treated his crew with disrespect. As a result, no one enjoyed working for him, and he lost his job.

   **A** respectably

   **B** respect

   **C** respectable

   **D** respectful

3. **What does the word *work* mean in this question?**

   Do you know when Luis starts work?

   **A** the job you do to earn money

   **B** the place where you have a job

   **C** to use and control something

   **D** something that you make or do

4. **Which of these words means "the state of being active?"**

   **A** actively

   **B** activity

   **C** inactive

   **D** activating

5. **Which of these sentences means that Brooke missed work last week?**

   **A** Brooke didn't go to work.

   **B** Brooke was late to work.

   **C** Brooke was sad because she couldn't see her friends at work.

   **D** Brooke didn't reach her goals at work.

6. **Which word from the passage means about the same as *rules*?**

   The employee handbook describes the company's expectations for good employees. It focuses on the dress code and policies about appropriate conduct and behavior.

   **A** handbook

   **B** focuses

   **C** policies

   **D** conduct

7. **Answer the following question.**

   How can you demonstrate integrity at work?

   **A** Tell the truth.

   **B** Tell people about your hobbies.

   **C** Disagree with your coworkers.

   **D** Play team sports.

8. **Which word best completes the passage?**

   When the water pipe broke, water went everywhere. Nobody knew what to do. But Angela just used her _____ and turned off the water.

   **A** honesty

   **B** hobbies

   **C** attitude

   **D** common sense

*What advice would you give someone who posts comments about his job and coworkers on social media? Write your answer on a separate sheet of paper. Use at least six words you learned in this unit. Circle the vocabulary words you use.*

*Check your answers beginning on page 105.*

# 6 Serving on a Team

## VOCABULARY

Read these words from the passage. Check the words you know.

- [ ] collaborate
- [ ] dispute
- [ ] divide
- [ ] effective
- [ ] flexible
- [ ] individual
- [ ] motivate
- [ ] opinion
- [ ] responsibility
- [ ] role
- [ ] teamwork
- [ ] volunteer

**Like players on a sports team, employees in a workplace work together to succeed.**

Picture a team of five basketball players. What if each one played as an **individual** instead of as part of the team? The team would probably not do very well. The players would likely have a hard time—both with scoring and with stopping the other team from getting points. The same idea applies to the workplace. **Teamwork** is essential for success in most businesses.

### What is teamwork?

When you work as a member of a team, you **collaborate** and work toward a common goal. Each person on the team brings his or her own set of skills. On an **effective** team, tasks can be **divided** according to the strengths and weaknesses of team members. Each person on the team contributes.

### How can teamwork be useful?

Working on a team can **motivate** you. For example, knowing that others depend on you may help you to meet deadlines. Also, a good team can do better work than most individuals who work alone. Teammates provide feedback, and that feedback can alert you to changes you could make to improve your work.

### How can you be a good team member?

You may have heard the term "team player." A team player is a person who works well on a team and helps the team succeed. Sometimes you may lead the team. At other times, you may play the **role** of group member.

To be a good member of a team, be **flexible** when you are asked to take on work. **Volunteer** for tasks. In addition, take **responsibility** and do your share of the work.

Sometimes, people on a team don't agree. It's important to deal with **disputes** and find solutions. Keep an open mind and listen to the **opinions** of others. If your team can't solve its disagreements, it will have trouble reaching its goals.

*What other words about teamwork do you know? Write them here.*

_____    _____    _____

# 1. Vocabulary Focus

*Complete each sentence with a word from the list.*

| collaborate | dispute | divide | effective | flexible | individual |
| motivate | opinion | responsibility | role | teamwork | volunteer |

1. When you _____ someone, you make the person want to work hard and do something.

2. When two or more people _____, they work together to get something done.

3. A _____ is the part or position someone has in an activity.

4. A person who is _____ is willing to change in a new situation.

5. When you _____ to do something, you offer to do it without someone else making you do it.

6. A _____ is an argument or a disagreement.

7. When two or more people work together to get something done, it is called _____.

8. When you take _____ for something, you agree to be in charge of it and to make decisions about it.

9. When you _____ a project, you split it into smaller parts.

10. If something is _____, it is successful and works well.

11. One person who acts alone is an _____.

12. An _____ is what someone thinks or feels about something. It is not a fact.

> The word *role* is pronounced like *roll*, but the two words have very different meanings. For example, *Rick's* <u>role</u> *in the bakery is to* <u>roll</u> *out the dough for* <u>rolls</u>. When you write, check that you are using the correct word.

# 2. Use the Vocabulary

*Write about a time when you used teamwork to get something done. Use at least three words from the vocabulary list. Circle the words you use.*

_____

_____

_____

# 3. Work With New Vocabulary

*Answer the questions. Then compare answers with a partner.*

1. What are some things a team can do to be **effective**?

_____

The word *role* can also mean the part an actor has in a movie or play.

2. Who has a more difficult **role**: the leader of a team, or a team member?

_____

3. What are some ways you can deal with a **dispute** with a coworker?

_____

4. Describe how **teamwork** can help a sports team.

_____

5. Describe a time when you have **collaborated** with others.

_____

People can volunteer to do something at work, but they can also volunteer in their communities. This means they do work to help others without getting paid for it.

6. What kinds of jobs or tasks would you be willing to **volunteer** for?

_____

7. Describe something you have **responsibility** for.

_____

8. Should workers always share their **opinions** with their bosses or managers? Explain why or why not.

_____

9. Think of a big project you have done or been part of. How was the project **divided**?

_____

10. Should police be **flexible** when people break the law? Explain why or why not.

_____

11. What are some things that could **motivate** a worker to do a good job?

_____

12. Do you prefer to work as an **individual** or as part of a team? Explain why.

_____

# 4. Prefixes col-, com-, con-

**The prefixes col, com, and con mean "with" or "together." For example, the word *collaborate* means "to work together."**

*Complete each sentence with a word from the list.*

| colleagues | collect | communicate | compromise | conference | confirmed |
| --- | --- | --- | --- | --- | --- |

1. Your _____ are the people you work with.

2. People on a team need to _____, so all members know what they are expected to do.

3. Eva's job on the team was to _____ information from customers and use it to write a report.

4. The manager _____ what he said earlier: the project must be finished in two weeks.

5. We went to a _____ where we learned about new technology.

6. Sometimes team members must _____, or give up something they want in order to get along with others.

# 5. Suffixes -able, -ible

**The suffixes –able and –ible mean "can be done" or "able to be." Most words that end in –able and –ible are adjectives.**

*Read each sentence. Write the meaning of the underlined word.*

1. Joyce is <u>responsible</u> for leading the team.

   responsible: _____

2. Kevin is <u>reliable</u> and always finishes his work on time.

   reliable: _____

3. My boss said I did an <u>incredible</u> job on the project.

   incredible: _____

4. Lily is <u>capable</u> of working on her own or as part of a team.

   capable: _____

5. Betsy is <u>available</u> to meet at 9 AM.

   available: _____

6. Tanya came up with a <u>possible</u> solution to the dispute.

   possible: _____

It can be hard to know which spelling to use if you are writing words with –able and –ible. If you remove the suffix and have a complete word, the word usually ends with –able. For example, remove the suffix from *dependable* and you have the word *depend*. Since *depend* is a word, it takes the suffix –able. Remove the suffix from *terrible* and you have *terr*, which is not a complete word. *Terrible* takes –ible.

# 6. Compound Words

**Most compounds that are written as one word can be found in a dictionary. Some compounds that are written as two words with a space between them are not in the dictionary. For these compounds, you will need to look up both words in order to figure out the meaning.**

*Complete each sentence with a compound word from the list.*

| conference room | deadline | newsletter | problem-solving | team leader |
|---|---|---|---|---|

1. The team needed to finish the project by the _____, which was two weeks away.

2. Vicki was responsible for getting the _____ written and printed.

3. The _____ at Doug's company has a large table and 12 chairs.

4. The _____ manages the team and makes sure team members do their jobs.

5. Teams must use _____ skills to deal with disputes and disagreements.

# 7. Context Clues: Synonyms and General Clues

**When you read a word that you don't know, look for clues that can help you figure out the meaning. You can look for general clues, such as how the word is used in the sentence and what the topic of the sentence is. You can also look for synonyms, or words that have a similar meaning.**

*Write the synonym for each boldfaced word.*

Teamwork is **essential** in the workplace. It is very important in meeting a business's goals. The **manager** of a team must understand each team member's strengths. This knowledge helps the person in charge to **assign** jobs. For example, a manager might give someone a **task** like working the cash register because she had good math skills. Team members must also **cooperate** with one another. Teams that work well together put the interests of the team first. Team members **depend** on each other to complete tasks, and they rely on one another to communicate about problems.

1. essential: _____

2. manager: _____

3. assign: _____

4. tasks: _____

5. cooperate: _____

6. depend: _____

# 8. Parts of Speech and the Dictionary

**When you look up a word in the dictionary, first find the entry. Then see if the word is listed more than once. If the same word is listed more than once, find the entry for the correct part of speech (for example, noun, verb, adverb, adjective). If the word has more than one meaning, the meanings will usually be numbered. Read through all the meanings to find the one that makes sense.**

*Look up each boldfaced word in a dictionary. Write the part of speech and the definition that matches how the word is used in the sentence.*

1. A team leader should be **clear** about what the tasks are and who will complete each one.

   _____  _____

2. Margaret has **experience** working in restaurants.

   _____  _____

3. It can be difficult to **express** your opinion to other team members.

   _____  _____

4. Patty has too much work. She needs to **delegate** some of it to other people on the team.

   _____  _____

5. Keila's new **project** is planning how to organize the products in the store.

   _____  _____

# 9. Multiple-Meaning Words

**A word can have more than one meaning. Think about a word's context to figure out the correct meaning.**

*Look at each underlined word. Circle the letter of the best definition.*

1. Minnie's team met its sales <u>goal</u> for July.
   a. a point scored in a sport
   b. something you want to do or achieve

2. We can <u>solve</u> the problem of long checkout lines by hiring more cashiers.
   a. to find a way to deal with a problem
   b. to find the answer to a mystery

3. The team leader <u>divided</u> the task into two parts.
   a. made people disagree
   b. split into parts

4. Adam knows how to <u>operate</u> the machines in the warehouse.
   a. to do surgery on a body
   b. to make a machine work

5. The shop wants to improve the <u>quality</u> of the goods it makes.
   a. the standard for how good something is
   b. a feature of something

# Unit 6 Review

*Complete each paragraph with words from the list.*

| assigned | deadline | divide | individual | project | role |
|---|---|---|---|---|---|

Al, Sara, and Ray are in the same history class. Their teacher (1) _____ them to work on a group (2) _____ together. The three students met after class to plan and talk about how to (3) _____ the work. They started by looking at the (4) _____, which was three weeks away. Then they discussed what (5) _____ each person would have. Each (6) _____ was given a part of the project to work on. They agreed to meet again in a week to see how things were going.

| delegates | manager | responsible | tasks | teamwork | volunteer |
|---|---|---|---|---|---|

Sharon, Anita, Reggie, and Don all work the night shift at Fresh Market. They use (7) _____ to make sure the store is ready for business in the morning. Sharon is the (8) _____. She is (9) _____ for making sure that everything gets done. Sharon (10) _____ different jobs to her team members. For example, the store must be cleaned, shelves must be filled with food, and food must be displayed. Some (11) _____, like mopping the floor, are not very popular. Anita will often (12) _____ to do less popular jobs like cleaning. She wants to be a team player and help the team succeed, even if it means doing jobs she doesn't enjoy.

| communicate | dispute | flexible | goals | opinions |
|---|---|---|---|---|

Sometimes people working on a team disagree on the best way to meet the team's (13) _____. People have different (14) _____ or views about who should do work or how work should be done. When there is a (15) _____, it's important to (16) _____ with other team members and deal with the disagreement right away. Try to be (17) _____ and keep an open mind. Focus on what's best for the team, not just for you.

*Read each question. Then circle the best answer.*

1. **Which definition of *collect* matches how the word is used in this sentence?**

   The workers <u>collect</u> information from each customer and enter it into the computer.

   **A** to ask for money for a certain purpose

   **B** a phone call in which the person getting the call must pay for it

   **C** to get and keep a certain type of item as a hobby

   **D** to gather things from different sources and put them together

2. **What is the meaning of *collaborated* in this sentence?**

   The cooks <u>collaborated</u> on a new menu and new dishes for the restaurant.

   **A** offered to do the job

   **B** disagreed about

   **C** worked together

   **D** split into parts

3. **Which of the following words means "people that work together"?**

   **A** colleagues

   **B** managers

   **C** disputes

   **D** opinions

4. **Which word best completes the sentence?**

   A good boss can _____ employees to work hard.

   **A** motivate

   **B** cooperate

   **C** operate

   **D** express

5. **What word or words in the passage mean about the same as *essential*?**

   The bakery's manager was concerned about the deadline. She said it was <u>essential</u> that the cakes be completely finished by 8 a.m. It was also very important that staff be available to serve customers.

   **A** concerned

   **B** completely finished

   **C** very important

   **D** available

6. **Which choice best completes the passage?**

   You can depend on Shelly to be on time and to do quality work. She is very _____.

   **A** possible

   **B** reliable

   **C** available

   **D** flexible

7. **Which choice describes a person who leads a group?**

   **A** a problem solver

   **B** a team leader

   **C** an individual

   **D** a colleague

8. **Which meaning of *clear* matches how the word is used in this sentence?**

   Logan's manager gave him <u>clear</u> instructions about how to work the machine.

   **A** without clouds, smoke, or mist

   **B** easy to see through

   **C** easy to understand

   **D** without spots or marks

*Describe how a good team can work together to get something done. Write your answer on a separate sheet of paper. Use at least six words you learned in this unit. Circle the vocabulary words you use.*

*Check your answers on page 106.*

# 7 Setting and Achieving Goals

## VOCABULARY

Read these words from the passage. Check the words you know.

- ☐ accountable
- ☐ achieve
- ☐ challenging
- ☐ commitment
- ☐ define
- ☐ focus
- ☐ measure
- ☐ method
- ☐ obstacle
- ☐ progress
- ☐ realistic
- ☐ vary

*A goal is a dream with a deadline. —Napoleon Hill, American author*

**Setting goals is important in both your personal and your work life. Read about ways to set and reach goals.**

Do you have goals in your personal life, such as improving your fitness or buying a home? Work goals are equally important. What do you want to be doing one month, a year, and five years from now? Setting goals can help you succeed in the workplace.

In order to **achieve** your goals, you must have a plan. You can't say "I want that" and expect to be successful. The SMART **method** can help you set goals. Each letter of the word *smart* stands for a guideline you can use to shape your plan.

- Specific: A specific goal is clear and well **defined**. Goals should not be vague, like "I want a better job." Instead, they should be precise, like "I will become a team leader."

- Measurable: You should be able to **measure** your success. Use exact amounts and dates when you set your goals. That way, you can check your **progress**.

- Achievable: Your goal should be something you can achieve. It should be **challenging** rather than easy, but also **realistic** for your situation. For example, most people would be incapable of reaching a goal to earn a million dollars next year.

- Relevant: Relevant goals **focus** on your career and interests. Your goals should matter to you. You may need to reflect on what's important in your life.

- Time-based: You should have a deadline for achieving a goal. Time frames for different goals will **vary** depending on how complex they are.

Think about your long-term goals. Then figure out short-term goals that will help you reach the long-term ones. After you have decided on goals, write them down and share them with someone. Writing and discussing your goals shows your **commitment** to them and can keep you **accountable**.

You might face **obstacles** while working toward your goals. For your best chance at success, try to identify and plan for possible obstacles.

*What other words about setting goals do you know? Write them here.*

_____  _____  _____

# 1. Vocabulary Focus

*Write each word from the list beside its definition.*

| | | | | | |
|---|---|---|---|---|---|
| accountable | achieve | challenging | commitment | define | focus |
| measure | method | obstacle | progress | realistic | vary |

_____  1. to give special attention to something

_____  2. the attitude of someone who works very hard to do or support something

_____  3. to judge something against a standard

_____  4. to show or describe something or someone clearly and completely

_____  5. responsible for your decisions and actions

_____  6. possible to do or achieve

_____  7. difficult

_____  8. the process of getting closer to a goal

_____  9. something that makes it difficult for you to achieve a goal

_____  10. a way of doing something

_____  11. to change depending on the situation

_____  12. to complete something successfully

> The word *challenging* can be an adjective: for example, *There was a challenging question on the math test.* Its root word is *challenge*, which can mean "a difficult task" or "to test someone's skills."

# 2. Use the Vocabulary

*Tell about some things you can do to set effective goals. Use at least three words from the vocabulary list. Circle the words you use.*

_____

_____

_____

_____

_____

# 3. Work With New Vocabulary

*Answer the questions. Then compare answers with a partner.*

1. What do you find **challenging** about your job or your schoolwork? Explain your answer.

   _____

2. Describe a goal that you are making **progress** toward.

   _____

3. Should politicians be **accountable** to voters? Explain your answer.

   _____

4. Describe a **realistic** personal goal for you. Why is your goal realistic?

   _____

The word *define* can also mean "to tell the meaning of a word."

5. How would you **define** what makes a TV show or movie good?

   _____

6. What kinds of **obstacles** do people face when they look for jobs?

   _____

7. What are some things that **vary** in your appearance?

   _____

8. How do you feel when you **achieve** a goal? Explain why.

   _____

In the word *measure*, the letter *s* makes the *zh* sound. This is the same sound you hear in *Asia* or *usual*.

9. How do you **measure** success at work?

   _____

10. Would you rather **focus** on work or getting an education? Why?

    _____

11. Describe two things that you have made a **commitment** to. How do you show your commitment?

    _____

12. Describe the **method** you would use to teach someone the main language you speak.

    _____

# 4. Prefixes *il-*, *im-*, *in-*, *ir-*

The prefixes *il-*, *im-*, *in-*, and *ir-* mean "not." These prefixes are added to the beginning of adjectives (words that describe), and they give those adjectives an opposite meaning. For example, *correct / incorrect*.

*Write the definition of the underlined word in each sentence.*

1. It was <u>impossible</u> for Tina to learn Chinese in a month, so she changed her goal.

   _____

2. The team was <u>incapable</u> of finishing by the deadline, so they asked for more time.

   _____

3. When Nina reviewed her goals, she saw that some of them were <u>irrelevant</u>.

   _____

4. Some dates in Richard's job application were <u>inaccurate</u>, so he had to correct them.

   _____

5. The school started a new program to teach <u>illiterate</u> parents how to read and write.

   _____

6. Some people get <u>impatient</u> when they try to achieve long-term goals.

   _____

> ● In some words, the prefixes *in-* and *im-* mean "in" or "into," as in the words *import* and *inside*. If you read a word that begins with *in-* or *im-*, you may need to use context clues to figure out the meaning.

# 5. Suffix *-ness*

The suffix *-ness* means "state or quality of." The suffix *-ness* is added to adjectives to make nouns. For example, *sad* (adjective) / *sadness* (noun).

*Complete each sentence with a word from the list.*

| awareness | correctness | greatness | preparedness | willingness |

1. Pete's _____ to learn new skills has helped him get better jobs.

2. One of the company's goals is to improve its disaster _____. The company wants to be ready in case of floods, tornados, and hurricanes.

3. The company president said that setting challenging goals can help the company achieve _____ and be an industry leader.

4. Having _____ of your goals means that you focus on them and check your progress.

5. When you apply for a job, the _____ of your resume and application matters. You don't want any errors.

> ● The suffix *-ness* is often added to words that describe feelings, such as *happy*, *sad*, *lonely*; and to ideas or concepts, such as *dark*, *good*, *messy*.

# 6. Compound Words

In most compounds, the second word carries most of the compound's meaning. For example, a *classroom* is a kind of room, not a kind of class.

**A compound word is two or more words that are put together but that have one meaning. A compound acts a single concept or idea, even if it is written as two words, like** *post office.*

*Write the compound word that matches each clue. Use words from the list.*

| long-term | milestone | roadblock | short-term | time frame | workplace |
|-----------|-----------|-----------|------------|------------|-----------|

_____ 1. lasting for a short period of time

_____ 2. a place, such as an office or factory, where people work

_____ 3. a place where police block a road to check traffic, or an obstacle that stops a plan

_____ 4. a period of time in which a project will be completed

_____ 5. lasting for a long period of time

_____ 6. an important event or step in a plan; also a stone along a road that shows how many miles to the next town

# 7. Context Clues: Antonyms

The following words may show that a writer is contrasting two things: *but, not, rather than, on the other hand, in contrast, instead, however, unlike.* If you see these words, the writer may be using antonyms.

**To figure out an unknown word, you can look for antonyms, words with an opposite or contrasting meaning.**

*Read each sentence. Underline words or phrases with the opposite or contrasting meaning to the boldfaced word. Then write the definition of the boldfaced word.*

1. The goals you set should be specific rather than **general**.

   _____

2. Judith's long-term goal was **complex**, but her short-term goals were simple.

   _____

3. Fred set clear work goals for himself. Antonio, on the other hand, wrote goals that were **vague**.

   _____

4. Setting goals and working to achieve those goals can be the difference between success and **failure**.

   _____

5. At the beginning of the year, the company **displayed** its goals for everyone to see. However, it hid the results when it didn't achieve its goals at the end of the year.

# 8. Parts of Speech and the Dictionary

**To figure out the meaning of a word, look at how it is used in the sentence. If you look up the word in the dictionary, make sure you are reading the definition for the correct part of speech.**

*Look up each boldfaced word in a dictionary. Write the part of speech and the definition that matches how the word is used in the sentence.*

1. Try to **post** your work goals where you will see them often.

   _____ _____

2. Your interests should **shape** your goals.

   _____ _____

3. Audrey made a **complete** list of the goals she wants to achieve this year.

   _____ _____

4. After you set goals, think about what problems you might **face**.

   _____ _____

5. It was a **challenge** to get employees to write down their goals.

   _____ _____

# 9. Multiple-Meaning Words

**Some words have more than one meaning. To figure out the correct meaning, look at how the word is used in the sentence. You can also think about the topic and look at nearby words for clues.**

*Look at each underlined word. Circle the letter of the best definition.*

1. You can get <u>support</u> from friends and family to help you reach personal goals.
   a. approval and help
   b. a thing that holds something up and stops it from falling

2. <u>Share</u> and discuss your goals with people you trust. This shows your commitment.
   a. divide between people
   b. tell other people your ideas and feelings

3. Before you set goals, <u>reflect</u> on what's important to you.
   a. think deeply about something
   b. show an image of something in a mirror

4. Some research <u>shows</u> that setting goals helps people achieve more at work.
   a. makes something clear
   b. lets someone see

5. After you set goals, <u>review</u> them often and check your progress.
   a. write an opinion about
   b. look at again

*Read the paragraph. Circle the word or words that best complete each sentence.*

At the start of the year, Emily made a (1) *complete / vague* list of the goals she wanted to (2) *show / achieve*. Emily had a (3) *long-term / roadblock* goal of starting her own business in five years. At first she thought opening her own business would be (4) *inaccurate / impossible*. But Emily had a (5) *weakness / willingness* to work hard toward her goals. She (6) *posted / shaped* the list on the wall at home so that she could see it and keep her goals in mind.

*Read the list of tips about setting goals. Then complete the tips with words from the list.*

| accountable | awareness | define | face | general |
|---|---|---|---|---|
| measure | method | obstacles | progress | share |

## Tips for Setting Goals

Setting goals can help you succeed. Having an (7) _____

of where you want to be can help you get there. What's a good way to set goals?

Try using the SMART (8) _____. This system can help you

(9) _____ your goals clearly and make them useful.

- Goals should be specific. If they are too (10) _____,

  you won't have enough direction.

- You should be able to (11) _____ your movement toward your goals, so be

  precise. Use numbers when possible so that you can check your (12) _____.

- Discuss your goals and (13) _____ them with people you trust.

  Talking to others about your goals can help you be (14) _____.

- Think about (15) _____ that might make it hard to achieve your goals.

  What problems will you (16) _____?

  Plan ahead so that you don't lose sight of your goal.

*Read each question. Then circle the best answer.*

1. **Which definition of *reflect* matches how the word is used in this sentence?**

   At the end of the year, many people reflect on what they achieved.

   **A** to show or be a sign of something

   **B** to send back heat, light, or sound from a surface

   **C** to show the image of something on a flat surface

   **D** to think about carefully

2. **What does *vary* mean in this sentence?**

   The length of time you need to complete a goal can vary depending on the goal.

   **A** to prove or make clear

   **B** to be difficult to do

   **C** to change or be different

   **D** to describe in detail

3. **Which of the following words means "the state or condition of being correct"?**

   **A** correction

   **B** incorrect

   **C** correctness

   **D** overcorrect

4. **Which choice best completes the sentence?**

   Bella's _____ for reaching her goal of becoming a store manager is five years.

   **A** time frame

   **B** short-term

   **C** roadblock

   **D** long-term

5. **Which word from the passage means about the same as *challenging*?**

   Set challenging goals for yourself. If your goals are too easy, you may not feel motivated. A difficult goal helps you to work harder and focus on important tasks.

   **A** easy

   **B** motivated

   **C** difficult

   **D** important

6. **Which choice best completes the passage?**

   Goals that are _____ will be hard to measure. Instead, goals should be specific.

   **A** vague

   **B** realistic

   **C** complete

   **D** illiterate

7. **Which choice is an example of a workplace?**

   **A** a factory

   **B** a goal

   **C** an awareness

   **D** a commitment

8. **Which meaning of *review* matches how the word is used in this sentence?**

   Take time to review your goals and check your progress.

   **A** to write a report about a book or movie in which you give an opinion

   **B** to look at or examine carefully

   **C** to look at notes before you take a test

   **D** to look at and describe past events

*Describe a work-related goal you have and the steps you plan to take to reach your goal. Write your answer on a separate sheet of paper. Use at least six words you learned in this unit. Circle the vocabulary words you use.*

*Check your answers on page 106.*

# 8 Understanding Performance Reviews

## VOCABULARY

Read these words from the passage. Check the words you know.

- ☐ compare
- ☐ critical
- ☐ defensive
- ☐ evaluate
- ☐ improve
- ☐ monitor
- ☐ objective
- ☐ performance
- ☐ performance appraisal
- ☐ probation
- ☐ promotion
- ☐ supervisor

### Abbreviation

HR (Human Resources)

**An evaluation can help you know what you do well and where you need to improve.**

A **performance appraisal** is a way for a manager to **evaluate** your job **performance**, or how you are doing at your job. Each company has its own way of evaluating employees. The process can help workers **improve** and let them know when they're doing well.

### Kinds of Performance Appraisals

There are different kinds of performance reviews. When you first start a job, you may be on **probation**. A probationary period can last weeks or months. This is a kind of trial period. The employer makes sure you can handle the job duties. Your **supervisor** usually **monitors** how well you complete certain tasks. At the end of the period, you continue as a regular employee or are let go.

Regular employees usually get evaluated once a year. In some companies, the review happens on your work anniversary. In other companies, all employees are reviewed around the same time.

### At the Performance Appraisal

Usually a supervisor writes an evaluation and discusses it with you. In some companies, the human resources department is part of the process. In the evaluation, the supervisor rates how well you met **objectives**. Sometimes the objectives are tied to goals set the previous year.

Supervisors may score employees to **compare** them to others and to company standards.

The supervisor meets with you to discuss strengths and areas needing improvement. The results of the evaluation may be used to decide who should get a **promotion** or a raise and who needs more training. A manager may develop an action plan for an employee who needs to improve.

### Preparing for the Evaluation

An evaluation can be stressful, but the process can help both you and the company meet goals. The best way to prepare is to work toward your goals all year, not just right before your review. You may have a chance to do a self-evaluation. If so, highlight what you have accomplished. If your supervisor is **critical** during the review, don't overreact or be **defensive**. Instead, focus on how you can do better.

*What other words about job evaluations do you know? Write them here.*

_____  _____  _____

# 1. Vocabulary Focus

*Write the word that completes each sentence.*

| compare | critical | defensive | evaluate |
| improve | monitor | objective | performance |
| performance appraisal | probation | promotion | supervisor |

To figure out word meanings, look for roots that you know. Do you recognize the roots in *defensive*, *performance*, and *promotion*?

1. A person who is in charge of another person and checks the person's work is a

   _____

2. When you _____ two or more people, you examine how they are alike and different.

3. An _____ is something you are trying to do or achieve.

4. A person who is _____ points out what's wrong or shows disapproval of something.

5. A _____ is a review, usually done once a year, of how well an employee is doing his or her job.

6. When you _____ something, you form an opinion about its value, quality, or usefulness.

7. A _____ is a move to a better or more important job in a company.

8. The period of time when a company trains and tests a new employee is called

   _____.

9. When you _____, you get better at something.

10. When you are _____, you behave in a way that shows you think someone is criticizing you.

11. A person's _____ at work is how well or how badly he does his job.

12. When you _____ something, you watch it and check how it changes over time.

# 2. Use the Vocabulary

*How are performance appraisals useful for companies? Use at least three words from the vocabulary list in your answer. Circle the words you use.*

_____

_____

_____

# 3. Work With New Vocabulary

*Answer the questions. Then compare answers with a partner.*

1. Give some examples of things a supervisor might be **critical** of.

   _____

2. Why might a company **compare** two workers?

   _____

3. How often do you think companies should do **performance appraisals**? Explain your answer.

   _____

4. If you were going to **evaluate** a used car before buying it, what would you look at?

   _____

5. Is getting a **promotion** a good or bad thing? Explain your answer.

   _____

6. Why might a company require a **probation** period for new workers?

   _____

7. When might an employee feel **defensive**? Give two examples.

   _____

8. What skills or qualities should a good **supervisor** have?

   _____

9. What are some ways you can **improve** as a student?

   _____

The word *performance* can also mean an activity that a person or a group does to entertain an audience.

10. What happens to someone who has poor **performance** at work?

    _____

11. What are some things that a person might need to **monitor** closely?

    _____

12. What personal **objectives** do you have?

    _____

## 4. Prefix over-

**The prefix over- can mean "too much" or "above." The prefix over- can be added to many nouns, verbs, and adjectives. For example, *overload, overeat, overdue*.**

*Write the definition of the underlined word in each sentence.*

1. Jade was <u>overdue</u> for her performance appraisal. The last one was 14 months ago.

   _____

2. Edgar <u>oversees</u> a team of nine people and must review each person.

   _____

3. Don't <u>overlook</u> any of your accomplishments when you have your annual review.

   _____

4. Sofia's boss <u>overreacted</u> when Sofia missed her monthly sales goal by just a few dollars.

   _____

5. She <u>overestimated</u> how many projects she could complete last year.

   _____

6. After some workers quit, the remaining employees felt <u>overworked</u>.

   _____

> The prefix *under-* is the opposite of *over-*. It means "not enough" or "below." For example, *underweight, undercharge*.

## 5. Root *val*

**The root *val* can mean "worth; strength; health." For example, the word *value* can mean "how much something is worth."**

*Match each word to its definition. Write the correct letter. Use a dictionary if you are unsure of the meaning of a word.*

_____ 1. valuable      a. to judge how good or useful something is

_____ 2. valid      b. very useful or important

_____ 3. evaluate      c. equal in value

_____ 4. validate      d. to give a lower value or make something seem less valuable

_____ 5. equivalent      e. to prove that something is true or correct

_____ 6. devalue      f. based on what is true or acceptable

*Write a sentence using two of the words from the list above.*

7. _____

> Roots can be combined with other roots, prefixes, and suffixes to form words. When you don't know a word's meaning, look for any word parts that you do know. The parts can help you figure out the word's meaning.

# 6. Compound Words

Compound words that are written as a single word are usually listed in the dictionary. Some compounds that are made up of two or more separate words are not in the dictionary. You will need to think about the meaning of the individual words in order to figure them out.

**A compound word is two or more words that are put together but have one meaning. You can figure out the meaning of many compounds by looking at the individual words that make up the compound.**

*Complete each sentence with a compound word from the list.*

| action plan | highlight | human resources | one-sided | point of view | workload |
| --- | --- | --- | --- | --- | --- |

1. Mei's _____ is too heavy. She wants to hire more people to help her.

2. The _____ department helped Jen get the computer training she needed.

3. Steve's boss created an _____ to help Steve improve at work.

4. Gina thought her review was _____. She wanted to explain her views.

5. In his review, Joe disagreed with his supervisor's _____.

6. Some companies have you do a self-evaluation. If you get to evaluate yourself, be sure to _____ everything you have achieved during the year.

# 7. Context Clues: General Clues

**Look for clues that help you figure out the meaning of a word you don't know. The clues might be similar words, definitions of the word, or examples of the word.**

*Look for clues that help you understand each boldfaced word. Then write the word's definition.*

The word *advice* is an uncountable noun. The word stands for an idea that can't be counted. You do not use the articles *a* or *an* in front of *advice*. For example: *I asked for advice.* NOT: *I asked for an advice.*

1. Don't be afraid to ask for **advice** from coworkers. They can share opinions about what you should do to succeed at work.

   *Advice* is _____

2. You do not need to wait for your annual review to **discuss** job performance. You should talk to your supervisor throughout the year about how you are doing.

   To *discuss* means _____

3. Joe has been working at Smith Supplies for a long time. He acts as a **mentor** for the younger employees and helps them face challenges at work.

   A *mentor* is _____

4. The manager asked Keith to sign his review to **acknowledge** that they had met and talked about it.

   To *acknowledge* means _____

5. The manager asked Ted to **prioritize** tasks. His boss said it was more important to help customers than to unpack boxes.

   To *prioritize* means _____

# 8. Parts of Speech and the Dictionary

**Many English words can be used for more than one part of speech. For example:** *I know how to tie a tie.* **In this sentence, the first** *tie* **is a verb, and the second** *tie* **is a noun. A dictionary gives different definitions for each part of speech.**

*Look up each boldfaced word in a dictionary. Write the part of speech and the definition that matches how the word is used in the sentence.*

1. His **regular** duties include ordering supplies.

   _____  _____

2. Don't make **excuses** for being late; just get to work on time!

   _____  _____

3. Tiffany **handles** all the bills for the shop.

   _____  _____

4. Ellen will **rate** her team on how well they worked together.

   _____  _____

5. There are **certain** things you should not say to a manager during your review.

   _____  _____

> An adjective is a word that describes a person or thing. Dictionaries use the abbreviation *adj.* to label adjectives.

> In your dictionary, look at how the word *excuse* is pronounced when it is a noun and a verb. As a verb, *excuse* ends with the *z* sound. As a noun, it ends with the *s* sound.

# 9. Multiple-Meaning Words

**A word can have more than one meaning. For example, the past tense verb** *tied* **has two different meanings in these sentences:** *I tied my shoe. The Eagles tied the score.* **Use the context of the sentence to help you figure out the correct meaning of a word.**

*Look at each underlined word. Circle the letter of the best definition.*

1. The company will review all employees during a two-week period in November.
   a. a length of time
   b. a part of a school day

2. The manager said Joel needed to improve in two areas: computer skills and teamwork.
   a. parts of a town or country
   b. subjects or activities

3. The company hires workers on a trial basis. If they are not good matches, they are let go.
   a. a legal process to see if someone is guilty
   b. a process to test someone's performance

4. Emilio got a score of 5 out of 5 on each objective in his performance appraisal.
   a. a number of points earned
   b. the total points in a game

5. Helen did a good job this year, so she is getting a raise.
   a. an increase in pay
   b. to lift something up

*Read each paragraph. Circle the word or words that best complete each sentence.*

Paul works in the shipping department of a large store. This year, Paul feels very (1) *overworked / overdue*. There aren't as many employees as there were a year ago. This means Paul has to (2) *score / handle* more tasks than he used to. Paul decided to (3) *compare / discuss* the situation with his (4) *supervisor / promotion*. Paul's manager (5) *oversees / overlooks* all the workers in the shipping department.

Paul and his manager talked about Paul's (6) *probation / workload*. Paul was careful about what he said. He didn't want to sound too (7) *certain / critical*. The supervisor thanked Paul for sharing his (8) *point of view / excuses*. He agreed that there was too much work and let Paul know that his concerns were (9) *defensive / valid*. He also said that he would speak to (10) *a mentor / human resources* about hiring more employees.

*Complete the paragraph below with words from the list.*

| evaluates | monitors | objectives | period | probation | regular | trial |
|---|---|---|---|---|---|---|

Some companies put new employees on (11) _____. This means that the worker is hired on a

(12) _____ basis. The length of the (13) _____ can vary, for instance it

might be four weeks or three months. During this time, the employee's supervisor (14) _____

his or her work. The employee usually has to meet (15) _____ in order to keep the job. At the

end of the probationary period, the supervisor (16) _____ the employee. If the employee has

done well, he or she becomes a (17) _____ employee.

*Read each question. Then circle the best answer.*

1. **Which definition of *performance* matches how the word is used in this sentence?**

   Susan's <u>performance</u> was good last year. She met all of her sales goals.

   **A** the act of putting on a play or concert

   **B** how a person does when acting in a play or giving a concert

   **C** how well or badly a person does a job

   **D** how well a car or machine works

2. **What does *action plan* mean in this passage?**

   Judy's manager gave her an <u>action plan</u> for next year. Judy needs to answer calls more quickly and complete more sales.

   **A** a meeting between a worker and manager

   **B** the steps you must take to reach a goal

   **C** a review of how well a worker did

   **D** the act of hiring a worker

3. **What does *raise* mean in this sentence?**

   Dave got a good review, and his supervisor gave him a $1,000 <u>raise</u>.

   **A** a nicer office

   **B** a better job

   **C** an increase in pay

   **D** a lift to a higher level

4. **Which choice best completes the sentence?**

   Vince wasn't sure which project to do first. He needed to _____ his work.

   **A** prioritize

   **B** overlook

   **C** devalue

   **D** highlight

5. **Which words from the passage mean about the same as *improve*?**

   A performance appraisal can help you <u>improve</u>. It can help you understand what you do well and what you should continue doing. But it can also point out areas where you need to get better.

   **A** help you understand

   **B** continue doing

   **C** point out

   **D** get better

6. **Which choice best completes the passage?**

   Jesse is a _____ employee. Last year, he kept the company's customers happy and helped the company make more money.

   **A** defensive

   **B** valuable

   **C** certain

   **D** overworked

7. **What does it mean if you *overreact*?**

   **A** You do not react enough.

   **B** You react too strongly.

   **C** You act again.

   **D** You act in a play.

8. **Which meaning of *acknowledge* matches how the word is used in this sentence?**

   Please <u>acknowledge</u> that you have read your review by signing and dating it.

   **A** to wave to show that you see someone

   **B** to admit that something is true

   **C** to give thanks for something you get

   **D** to tell or show someone that a message has been received

*Describe what you learned about performance appraisals. What can employees do to earn good evaluations? Write your answer on a separate sheet of paper. Use at least six words you learned in this unit. Circle the vocabulary words you use.*

*Check your answers beginning on page 106.*

# 9 Understanding Employee Benefits

## VOCABULARY

Read these words from the passage. Check the words you know.

- ☐ accrue
- ☐ contribute
- ☐ disability
- ☐ enroll
- ☐ insurance
- ☐ match
- ☐ matters
- ☐ personal days
- ☐ qualify
- ☐ retirement
- ☐ Social Security
- ☐ vested

## Abbreviation

PTO (paid time off)

**Along with your salary, your employer will provide you with benefits. Benefits vary from company to company. For many people, health care coverage is the most important benefit.**

When you start a new job, you learn about your benefits, or the extra items that an employer offers full-time employees. The law requires your employer to provide certain benefits, such as **Social Security**. In addition, many companies offer other benefits. These usually include paid vacation time, health **insurance**, and a **retirement** plan. Make sure that you take advantage of everything that is offered and that you **enroll** in everything you should.

### Health Insurance

Employee benefits are designed to improve your quality of life. For example, health insurance helps cover the high cost of medical care. If you work fulltime, you probably **qualify** for health care coverage. In most cases, you pay for part of your health benefits, and your employer pays for part. Employers may also offer more than one plan. Find the plan that works best for you.

### Retirement Plans

The sooner you start planning for your retirement, the better. Many companies offer a 401(k) plan to which employees **contribute** money, and employers **match** that contribution up to a certain percent of the salary. Try to contribute at least up to your employer's match. The money you put into your plan is deducted, or taken out of your paycheck, *before* income taxes are taken out. If you leave a company before you are **vested** in the 401(k) program, you lose the money your employer put in. It usually takes five years to become vested. But of course you keep the money you put in.

### Time Off

Generally, you **accrue** a specific number of paid vacation and sick days for each month you work. These days add up over time. You may also get paid holidays and **personal days**. Personal days are paid days you can take off to take care of personal or private **matters**.

There are many other benefits—**disability** insurance if you're unable to work, vision insurance, childcare—that your employer may offer. Learn everything you can about them and decide if they are right for you.

*What other words about benefits at work do you know? Write them here.*

_____    _____    _____

# 1. Vocabulary Focus

*Write each word from the list beside its definition.*

| accrue | contribute | disability | enroll |
|---|---|---|---|
| insurance | match | matters | personal days |
| qualify | retirement | Social Security | vested |

_____ 1. to pay an amount of money that is equal to another amount

_____ 2. the time in your life when you stop working

_____ 3. an agreement in which you make regular payments to a company that pays you if something bad happens

_____ 4. an illness or injury that limits your mental or physical abilities

_____ 5. a government program that provides benefits to retirees and other people in need

_____ 6. to join as a member in a group

_____ 7. having full ownership

_____ 8. to give to or be a part of something together with other people

_____ 9. time off from work for reasons other than illness or vacation

_____ 10. to grow or increase

_____ 11. to have the right

_____ 12. things you have to talk about or do

# 2. Use the Vocabulary

*Choose three of the vocabulary words. Define them in your own words.*

1. _____

2. _____

3. _____

*Share your definitions with a partner. Talk about them, and make suggestions for revising them. Rewrite your definitions and show them to your teacher.*

# 3. Work With New Vocabulary

*Write your answers. Then compare answers with a partner.*

1. List the different kinds of **insurance** you read about in order from most to least important to you. Explain your choices.

   _____

2. What are two benefits of **enrolling** in a health insurance plan at work?

   _____

3. You can **contribute** to your future by paying into a 401(k) plan at work. How can you contribute to your community and other people outside of work?

   _____

4. "The sooner you start planning for your **retirement**, the better." How can you start planning for your retirement today?

   _____

5. Explain why it's a good idea to **match** your employer's contribution to your 401(k).

   _____

6. Give three good reasons for taking a **personal day** off from work.

   _____

7. It generally takes five to eight years for an employee to become fully **vested** in an employer's 401(k) plan. Why do you think it takes so long?

   _____

8. Would you rather work for a company that allows you to **accrue** vacation time from one year to the next or for a company that makes you use your vacation time up every year? Why?

   _____

9. Should everyone have to pay into **Social Security**? Why or why not?

   _____

10. When is it OK to discuss personal **matters** at work?

    _____

11. Sometimes you have to work at a company for 90 or even 180 days before you **qualify** for benefits. Why do companies have this requirement?

    _____

12. Short-term **disability** insurance covers the first few weeks or months when you can't work. Long-term disability insurance starts paying after that and lasts much longer. Explain which one you think is more important to have and why.

    _____

## 4. Roots *bene, bon, boun*

**The roots *bene, bon* and *boun* mean "good; well." Read the definitions of these words with the roots *bene, bon* and *boun*.**

    **beneficial:** producing good or helpful results or effects
    **beneficiary:** a person who receives something good from someone else such as an inheritance
    **benefit:** to be useful or helpful to someone or something
    **bonus:** extra benefits, usually extra pay
    **bounty:** a very large amount of something

*Use one of the words from the list above to complete each sentence.*

1. Everyone who worked for the bookstore got a _____ check at the end of the year.

2. Regular exercise is _____ to your health. It's not always fun, but it is good for you.

3. There was a _____ of delicious food at the company holiday party. We contributed some of it to a local food bank.

4. The company's new health insurance options will _____ many employees.

5. Collin's daughter is the only _____ of his life insurance.

## 5. Suffix *-ment*

**The suffix *-ment* means "action; process" or "the result, goal, or method of an action." Words that end in *-ment* are nouns. For example, *to retire* means "to stop working because you have reached a certain age." *Retirement* is the time in your life after you retire.**

*Use a word from the list to complete each sentence. Check a dictionary if you don't know the meaning of a word.*

| advertisement | investment | payment | reimbursement | replacement |
|---|---|---|---|---|

1. If you enroll in a health plan before the 15th of a month, your coverage usually starts at the beginning of the next month, after you make your first _____.

2. Debra explained that contributing to a 401(k) is an excellent financial _____.

3. Barry saw an _____ online for a tech support job with great benefits.

4. Tuition _____ is a great employee benefit. Your employer pays for your continuing education if it is in an area related to the business.

5. When Gwen lost her insurance ID card, she got a _____ from the insurance company.

# 6. Compound Words

The best thing to do when you have a question about a compound word is to look it up in the dictionary.

**Open compound words have a space between the words, but when they are read together, they have a new meaning.**

*Complete each sentence with a compound word from the list.*

| childcare | flexible spending account | flextime |
|---|---|---|
| income tax | open enrollment | stock options |

1. Large companies may offer _____. You buy shares of the company at a discounted price so you can sell them when their value increases.

2. Another useful benefit is a _____ which helps you save money to pay for medical and daycare expenses.

3. A 401(k) is an excellent way to save for retirement, and you don't have to pay _____ on the money until you take it out of your account.

4. It makes sense that _____ is an important benefit for many working parents.

5. With _____, you work the usual number of hours, but you choose regular starting and finishing times that are better for you.

6. Once a year during _____, employees may change some of their benefits.

# 7. Context Clues: Definitions and General Clues

**When you read an unfamiliar word, you can check to see if the writer has explained it. You can also look at surrounding words for clues about the unfamiliar word.**

*Complete each sentence with a word from the list.*

| comprehensive | dependents | guarantee | premium | welfare |
|---|---|---|---|---|

1. Retirement plans _____, or promise, that you'll have an income after you stop working.

2. Trudy's company pays part of the _____ for her health insurance. She pays the rest of the money.

3. The state offers complete and _____ health and life insurance to all employees.

4. Lindsay's health insurance plan covers her and her _____. Of course, the family plan is more expensive than the employee-only plan.

5. Western Cable Services is concerned about the health and _____ of its employees, so it provides benefits to help them stay physically and mentally healthy.

# 8. Parts of Speech and the Dictionary

**To figure out the meaning of a word, look at how it is used in the sentence.**

*Look up each boldfaced word in a dictionary. Write the definition that matches how the word is used in the sentence.*

1. A flexible spending account can be used to pay childcare **costs**.

   definition: _____

2. I wonder if it **matters** that I have a new doctor. Will that change anything about my health insurance?

   definition: _____

3. Most employers offer paid **leave** for the death of a close family member.

   definition: _____

4. Quality medical insurance **benefits** both the employer and the employee.

   definition: _____

5. A large **firm** is more likely to provide comprehensive benefits than a small one.

   definition: _____

# 9. Multiple-Meaning Words

**When a word has multiple meanings, pick the meaning that works best in the context of the specific sentence.**

*Look at each underlined word. Circle the letter of the best definition.*

1. Howard doesn't know if his vision insurance <u>covers</u> glasses as well as visits to the eye doctor.
   a. to provide payment for
   b. to put one thing over another thing to protect, hide, or close it

2. Companies show that they <u>value</u> their employees by offering good benefits packages.
   a. to appreciate
   b. to judge

3. Lara and Ted <u>care</u> about getting comprehensive health insurance for their children.
   a. to feel affection for
   b. to be interested in

4. Rebecca gets two weeks paid vacation <u>time</u> and three paid personal days a year.
   a. a specific period in the past
   b. a period of seconds, minutes, hours, days, months, or years

5. Before you accept a new job, ask about the benefits <u>package</u>.
   a. a group of related things that go together
   b. a box or large envelope

# Unit 9 Review

*Complete the paragraphs. Use words from the lists.*

| contribute | firm | insurance | match | open enrollment | vested |
|---|---|---|---|---|---|

Last month was (1) _____ at Alton and Bowers, and many of the employees were interested

in learning what new benefits were available. There was a company meeting where everyone could ask questions.

Lamar was thinking about making some changes. The (2) _____ was offering several

new (3) _____ plans, including life and disability. He thought he might participate

in the 401(k) retirement program, too. It seemed like a good way to save money, and he would be fully

(4) _____ in five years. If he chose to (5) _____ three percent of his

salary, the company would (6) _____ his investment.

| accrue | childcare | costs | flexible spending account | personal days | qualify | value |
|---|---|---|---|---|---|---|

Carrie was looking for a (7) _____ plan that would help with

(8) _____ for her young son and with the family's medical bills.

As a fulltime employee, Darren was happy to (9) _____ for benefits for the first time. He

asked about the (10) _____ of the various health insurance plans because some were much

more expensive than others. He also wanted to understand the difference between vacation time, sick days, and

(11) _____.

The owners of Alton and Bowers (12) _____ their employees and offer the best benefits

package they can.

*Read each question. Then circle the best answer.*

1. **What does the word *care* mean in this question?**

   Do you <u>care</u> whether your insurance plan includes vision or not?

   **A** to take care of someone

   **B** to protect

   **C** to feel affection for

   **D** to be concerned about

2. **Complete the sentence.**

   When companies offer flextime, their employees can _____.

   **A** choose when they start and leave work

   **B** work from home

   **C** take time off from work

   **D** retire at a young age

3. **Graham is looking for insurance that will pay him if he gets hurt and can't work. Which choice best describes the kind of insurance Graham wants?**

   **A** retirement

   **B** life

   **C** disability

   **D** dental

4. **Which definition of *time* matches how the word is used in this sentence?**

   It took a long <u>time</u> for Mateo to decide which was the best plan for his family.

   **A** what is measured in minutes, hours, days, etc.

   **B** the period when a particular activity usually happens

   **C** a specific minute or hour shown on a clock

   **D** a specific event or experience

5. **Which word best completes the sentence?**

   Everyone knows that regular exercise has many _____ health effects.

   **A** benefit

   **B** beneficial

   **C** bonus

   **D** benevolent

6. **Which word from the passage means about the same as *enrolled*?**

   Jodie <u>enrolled</u> in the stock options plan at the tech company where she worked last year. She joined after she read the company's yearly report. She bought shares of stock every pay period.

   **A** worked

   **B** joined

   **C** read

   **D** bought

7. **Which word best completes the passage?**

   Denyse joined the 401(k) program at work. Both she and her employer make a monthly _____ to her account.

   **A** replacement

   **B** improvement

   **C** payment

   **D** reimbursement

8. **What does the word *package* mean in this sentence?**

   During open enrollment, Harrison signed up for a comprehensive benefits <u>package</u>.

   **A** a box or bag that things are packed in to be sold

   **B** a group of things that go together

   **C** a wrapper that covers something

   **D** a box that is sent by mail

*Think of all the different benefits you've read about. Which ones do you think are the most important? Write your answer on a separate sheet of paper. Explain your choices. Use at least six words you learned in this unit. Circle the vocabulary words you use.*

*Check your answers on page 107.*

# 10 Understanding Your Paycheck

$1,234.56

## VOCABULARY

Read these words from the passage. Check the words you know.

- ☐ allowances
- ☐ deductions
- ☐ dependent
- ☐ direct deposit
- ☐ federal
- ☐ gross pay
- ☐ net pay
- ☐ paycheck
- ☐ payroll cards
- ☐ paystub
- ☐ pay period
- ☐ withhold

### Abbreviations

FICA (Federal Insurance Contributions Act)

IRS (Internal Revenue Service)

YTD (year-to-date)

**Remember: you don't take home every dollar you earn. You have to pay taxes, and employers must pay them from your paycheck.**

In order to get paid when you start a new job, you will fill out several employment forms. When you complete a Form W-4, you determine how much of your salary your employer will **withhold** for taxes. The amount is based on how many **allowances** you claim. You get an allowance for yourself, one for your spouse, and one for each **dependent**.

You may be able to choose how the company pays you. The most traditional method of payment is a paper **paycheck**. But many employers also offer **direct deposit** and pay straight into your bank account. Other employers provide **payroll cards** and electronically load your payment onto a plastic card.

There are two parts to your paycheck—the paper check and the **paystub** that explains everything that is on your paycheck. The information on your paystub is usually listed in two columns. One is for this **pay period** ("current"), and one is for all of the pay periods since January 1 of this year ("year-to-date").

In both columns, you see your **gross pay**, or the total amount of money you earned. You also see your **net pay**, the amount of money that you get to take home *after* taxes and **deductions** are taken out. Net pay is the dollar amount on your paycheck. It is also known as take-home pay.

Your paystub shows all of your deductions. Your retirement savings plan, health plan, etc. are usually paid with pretax dollars. Then taxes such as **federal** income tax, Social Security, and Medicare (a federal health-care program) are deducted. Most states also collect state income tax. In some areas you must pay local taxes as well.

You are responsible for making sure that this information is correct. The best way to do this is to understand what is being withheld and what it is being used for. If you have questions about anything on your paystub, talk to your supervisor, someone in human resources, or your employer.

*What other words about paychecks, taxes, and deductions do you know? Write them here.*

_____  _____  _____

# 1. Vocabulary Focus

*Match each word with its definition. Write the correct letter.*

_____ 1. allowance

_____ 2. deductions

_____ 3. dependent

_____ 4. direct deposit

_____ 5. federal

_____ 6. gross pay

_____ 7. net pay

_____ 8. paycheck

_____ 9. payroll card

_____ 10. paystub

_____ 11. pay period

_____ 12. withholding

a. relating to our national government

b. the money you take home after taxes and other deductions

c. a check that your employer uses to pay your salary

d. the calendar days for which you are being paid

e. the money you make before taxes and deductions are taken out of your paycheck

f. A way of paying someone so that the money is sent directly into that person's bank account

g. a plastic card onto which your employer deposits your pay electronically

h. An amount of money that is set aside as non-taxable

i. the part of your paycheck that shows the details of what you earned and what was taken out

j. a person who relies on another person for financial support

k. money taken from your paycheck to pay for federal, state, and local income taxes

l. money taken from your paycheck to pay for your contributions to insurance, retirement, etc.

● It is also correct to write *paystub* as two words, *pay stub*.

# 2. Use the Vocabulary

*Parker's gross salary is $600 a week, but this isn't the amount on his paycheck. Explain why. Use at least three words from the vocabulary list. Underline the vocabulary words in your explanation.*

_____

_____

_____

_____

## 3. Work With New Vocabulary

*Answer the questions. Then compare answers with a partner.*

1. Name an advantage and a disadvantage of being paid with a **payroll card**.

   _____

2. If you started a new job today, how many **dependents** could you claim? Explain your answer.

   _____

3. Ben's father told him to keep all of his **paystubs** in a safe place. Why is that good advice?

   _____

4. If you wanted to determine a person's **net pay**, what information would you need to have?

   _____

5. Why does a company **withhold** money from its employees' paychecks?

   _____

6. Will you increase your take-home pay by taking as many **allowances** as possible or by taking as few as possible? Explain your thinking.

   _____

7. What are four things you can take as paycheck **deductions**?

   _____

8. Will your **gross pay** ever be lower than your take-home pay? Why or why not?

   _____

9. A pay period can be monthly. List two other examples of **pay periods**.

   _____

10. What do your **federal** taxes pay for? What about state and local taxes?

    _____

11. Why do you think most people prefer to be paid through **direct deposit**? Give three reasons.

    _____

12. How often would you like to receive your **paycheck**? Explain your answer.

    _____

# 4. Prefix *pre-*

**The prefix *pre-* means "before." The prefix *pre-* can come before a base word, as in *preview*. *Pre-* can also come before a word root that cannot stand alone without the prefix, as in *predict*.**

*The underlined word in each sentence starts with the prefix* pre-. *Write the definition of the underlined word. Use a dictionary to check your answers.*

1. Your net pay will be lower than your gross pay, so <u>prepare</u> yourself to see a lower number on your paystub.

   definition: _____

2. At Julianna's <u>previous</u> job, she was paid with a paper check. At her current job, she uses direct deposit.

   definition: _____

3. A payroll card is similar to a <u>prepaid</u> credit card.

   definition: _____

4. Contributions to a flexible spending account are deducted from your <u>pretax</u> income.

   definition: _____

5. The amount of money you pay in taxes is <u>predetermined</u> by how much money you make.

   definition: _____

# 5. Suffix *-al*

**The suffix *-al* means "having characteristics of." You can add the suffix *-al* to the end of some nouns or root words to make adjectives. For example, the noun *tradition* + *-al* = the adjective *traditional* and the root *dent* + *-al* = the adjective *dental*.**

*Read each sentence and circle the word that best completes it. If you don't know the meaning of a word, look it up.*

1. Paying taxes is not *accidental* / *optional*.

2. Does your new insurance plan include *dental* / *traditional* coverage?

3. It's your responsibility to make sure that the *personal* / *seasonal* information on your paycheck is current.

4. Paying into your 401(k) is a smart *financial* / *official* decision; it's paid with pretax dollars.

5. This is Gil's *original* / *economical* job description. His manager rewrote it when Gil was promoted.

6. After Jax and Mariah had children, they bought *additional* / *financial* insurance.

> If the base word ends in *e*, drop the *e* and add *-ial*, as in *finance* and *financial*.

*Add the suffix* -al *or* -ial *to these words. Then use each word in a sentence.*

7. nation _____

8. commerce _____

# 6. Compound Words

A compound word is formed when two or more words that can stand alone are joined to make a new word. If you know the meanings of the smaller words, you can often combine them into a single meaning for the compound.

*Write a compound word from the list to match each clue.*

| bonus pay | income tax | overtime pay | pay rate | payroll | taxable income |
| --- | --- | --- | --- | --- | --- |

_____  1. an employee's gross pay minus any pretax deductions

_____  2. how much an employee is paid, often listed by the hour

_____  3. money that employees and employers pay the government on their earnings

_____  4. the money hourly employees are paid for working more than their regular hours

_____  5. a list of employees and the amounts they are paid

_____  6. additional money employees are paid over their usual pay, usually at the end of the year

# 7. Context Clues: Definitions and Synonyms

The first word after the comma may be *or*. This lets you know that you are going to see another way to think about the unknown word.

**When you try to figure out the meaning of a word from its context, look for a word or phrase that defines or explains it. The word or words will probably be set off by commas. For example, the commas in this sentence tell you that *determine* and *figure out* mean about the same thing: *You can determine, figure out, your taxable income if you know how much is deducted from your gross pay.***

*Read each sentence. Look for context clues to help you figure out the meaning of the boldfaced word. Circle the word or words that define it.*

1. Your tax rate is based on your **annual**, or yearly, income.

2. Brielle uses direct deposit. Every pay period she gets a copy of her paycheck marked **non-negotiable**. She can't exchange it for money.

When people write *miscellaneous*, they often use the abbreviation *misc.*

3. **Miscellaneous**, mixed and different, deductions were taken out of Kara's paycheck for things like cleaning her uniform and buying her equipment.

4. Jeremy was surprised by all the things that **affect**, or influence, how much of his salary he ends up taking home.

5. It's a good idea to check that your taxes have been **calculated**, or determined mathematically, correctly.

6. If something seems wrong with your paycheck, **consult**, or get advice from, human resources or your manager.

# 8. Parts of Speech and the Dictionary

**A word may mean one thing when it's used as a noun. It may mean something else when it's used as an adjective or a verb. When you use a dictionary, you'll see all of the definitions of a word listed by their part of speech.**

*Look up each boldfaced word in a dictionary. Write the part of speech and the definition that matches how the word is used in the sentence.*

1. **List** all of your dependents so you can determine how many allowances you can take.

   _____  _____

2. The year-to-date column on your paystub allows you to **track** how much money you've made and how much you've paid in taxes.

   _____  _____

3. This year, Terrel is going to **file** taxes for the first time.

   _____  _____

4. Did Anna **check** her paystub before she went to human resources?

   _____  _____

5. Do you remember which **forms** you completed on Monday?

   _____  _____

> If you know the part of speech of an unfamiliar word, you understand how the word is used. Knowing this will help you figure out the meaning of the word.

# 9. Multiple-Meaning Words

**Many words have more than one meaning. They can be used in different ways depending on the surrounding words, or context.**

*Look at each underlined word. Circle the letter of the best definition.*

1. Ethan tries hard to <u>earn</u> the respect of his employees.
   a. to be paid for working
   b. to deserve

2. When Andrea started working, she opened up a savings <u>account</u>.
   a. an arrangement that lets you keep your money in a bank
   b. an arrangement when you use Internet or email services

3. Since his mother lives with him, Clark can <u>claim</u> her as a dependent.
   a. say that something is true when some people may say it is not true
   b. say that you have a legal right to something

4. Nora made a <u>statement</u> to her team explaining why she was leaving the firm.
   a. a document showing money you have received, spent, etc.
   b. something you say or write in an official way

5. With direct deposit, you can <u>access</u> your money right away.
   a. open or load something on the Internet
   b. to be able to use, enter, or get near

# Unit 10 Review

*Read each paragraph. Complete each sentence with a word from the list.*

| annual | deductions | dental | gross pay | income taxes | pay period |
|--------|-----------|--------|-----------|--------------|------------|

When Buddy was hired at WKRI Radio, he was offered an (1) _____, or yearly,

salary of $33,000. He was pretty happy when he calculated how much money he would make each

(2) _____. But he didn't consider that the $33,000 was his (3) _____,

or the total amount of money he would make before (4) _____ such as his

(5) _____ insurance and (6) _____.


| access | account | net pay | paycheck | payroll |
|--------|---------|---------|----------|---------|

Not surprisingly, Buddy was not happy when he got his first (7) _____. His

(8) _____ was lower than he had expected. He walked right down the hall to talk to

Stephanie in the (9) _____ department. She went online to (10) _____

his records and looked at Buddy's (11) _____ to find out what was confusing him.


| dependents | federal | financial | withholds |
|-----------|---------|-----------|-----------|

After talking to him for a while, Stephanie figured out what Buddy's problem was. She explained various

(12) _____ choices he could make. She advised him about increasing the number of

(13) _____ he claimed. She explained how (14) _____, state, and local

taxes affected his take-home pay. And Buddy learned that the difference between his gross pay and his net pay is

how much money his employer (15) _____.

*Read each question. Then circle the best answer.*

1. **Which words from the passage mean about the same as *calculated*?**

   Pehr thought there was a mistake on his last paycheck. He <u>calculated</u> his overtime pay and figured out his deductions and withholdings. But the numbers didn't make sense, so he met with JJ in the payroll department. They accessed his account online and found the problem.

   **A** thought

   **B** figured out

   **C** met with

   **D** accessed

2. **Which word describes something that relates to a particular person?**

   **A** personal

   **B** personnel

   **C** personality

   **D** personals

3. **Which description best describes *bonus pay*?**

   **A** extra money paid to an employee

   **B** money an employee can deposit directly

   **C** money an employee doesn't pay taxes on

   **D** extra money taken from an employee's salary

4. **Which word best completes the passage?**

   Sonny gets paid every two weeks. The first _____ was November 2 through November 13.

   **A** paycheck

   **B** net pay

   **C** statement

   **D** pay period

5. **Which word best completes the sentence?**

   Mary Beth paid into her 401(k) with _____ dollars.

   **A** previous

   **B** pretax

   **C** predetermined

   **D** prepared

6. **What does the word *check* mean in this sentence?**

   Our new <u>checks</u> have a lot of personal information on them.

   **A** a piece of paper that shows how much you owe for food in a restaurant

   **B** an examination to see that everything is right, good, or, safe

   **C** a piece of printed paper from your bank that you can use to pay for things

   **D** a small mark like this: ✓

7. **Saba was surprised when she saw her take-home salary after taxes. Which choice best describes what surprised Saba?**

   **A** her gross pay

   **B** her net pay

   **C** her pay rate

   **D** her payroll card

8. **Which definition of *allowance* best matches how the word is used in this sentence?**

   Vi pays her daughter a weekly <u>allowance</u> for working around the house.

   **A** money given to someone to pay their living expenses

   **B** an amount of something that you are allowed by rules or by law

   **C** money that can be earned without paying taxes

   **D** money that a parent regularly gives a child

*A good friend is starting her first job in two weeks. Explain what she should expect to see on her first paycheck. Write your answer on a separate sheet of paper. Circle the vocabulary words you use.*

*Check your answers beginning on page 107.*

# 11 Staying Safe at Work

## VOCABULARY

Read these words from the passage. Check the words you know.

- ☐ accident
- ☐ avoidable
- ☐ dangerous
- ☐ gear
- ☐ harm
- ☐ hazard
- ☐ ignore
- ☐ injury
- ☐ machine
- ☐ prevent
- ☐ safety
- ☐ warn

**Most people don't think about staying safe at work. But accidents can and do happen.**

Every job comes with possible **hazards**, which are things or actions that can **harm** people. It is important to understand the **safety** issues that affect your workplace. Learn how to stay safe at work and what to do if there is an **accident**.

### Workplace Hazards

Many work accidents are **avoidable**. To stay safe at work, you can watch for **dangerous** situations and avoid taking risks. Watch for signs that **warn** of danger, such as a slippery floor or a hot surface.

Know how to use tools and equipment safely. Being careless can result in **injuries** like burns, cuts, and falls. If an injury occurs, know where the first aid kit is and how to get help.

### Dress and Safety Gear

Wear clothes and shoes that are appropriate for your job. For example, high-heeled shoes or flip-flops are inappropriate for a construction job. Scarves, long hair, and loose shirtsleeves can be dangerous around **machines** with moving parts.

Many jobs require safety **gear** for protection. Be sure to wear proper gear. Examples of protective gear include gloves, safety goggles, work boots, and hard hats. In a noisy workplace, you may also need to protect your hearing.

### Fire Safety

Fires can occur in buildings, in vehicles, and at worksites. To reduce the risk of fire, keep work areas free of extra paper, trash, and flammable items. Keep equipment away from things that can burn. Know where the nearest fire extinguisher is for putting out small fires.

A fire can spread quickly, so don't **ignore** flames, smoke, or a fire alarm. Call 911 and leave the area immediately. Make sure you know where the emergency exits are, and don't use elevators during a fire.

### Report Hazards and Accidents

If you see something unsafe at work, report it right away. This can help **prevent** injuries. Anyone hurt at work should report injuries promptly. Injured workers have legal rights. They may be able to collect workers' compensation, a kind of insurance.

*What other words about job safety do you know? Write them here.*

_____  _____  _____

# 1. Vocabulary Focus

*Complete each sentence with a word from the list.*

| accident | avoidable | dangerous | gear | harm | hazard |
|---|---|---|---|---|---|
| ignore | injury | machine | prevent | safety | warn |

To figure out word meanings, look for base words inside longer words. What shorter words do you see in *avoidable*, *dangerous*, and *safety*?

1. If something is _____, you can stop it from happening.

2. The clothing or equipment that you need to do a certain activity is your _____.

3. An _____ is damage to a part of your body.

4. To _____ someone or something means to hurt or cause damage.

5. A _____ is a danger or a risk.

6. A _____ is a piece of equipment that you use to do a job. It uses power and has moving parts.

7. _____ is the state of being safe from danger.

8. An event that is not planned and that hurts someone is an _____.

9. When you _____ people, you tell them about a possible danger so that they can avoid it.

10. When you _____ something, you pay no attention to it or act like you did not see or hear it.

11. When you _____ something, you stop it from happening.

12. Something that is _____ is not safe. It could hurt you.

# 2. Use the Vocabulary

*Why should workers think about safety at work? Use at least three words from the vocabulary list. Circle the words you use.*

_____

_____

_____

_____

# 3. Work With New Vocabulary

*Answer the questions. Then compare answers with a partner.*

1. Would you **ignore** a person you care about? Explain your answer.

_____

2. What kinds of **machines** can you find in a kitchen?

_____

3. What things might a person do to cause an **accident**? Explain your answer.

_____

4. Is getting a cold or the flu **avoidable**? Explain your answer.

_____

5. Which person faces more **hazards** at work: a teacher or a firefighter? Explain your thinking.

_____

6. Name a job where workers need to wear special **gear**. What kind of gear do they wear?

_____

7. Would you work in a place that is **dangerous**? Why or why not?

_____

8. Can saying mean things to someone **harm** that person? Explain your answer.

_____

9. Would a weatherperson **warn** people about a sunny day? Explain your answer.

_____

10. What are some things you do to **prevent** illness?

_____

11. What could your school or job do to improve **safety**?

_____

12. What kinds of **injuries** would a person working in a fast-food restaurant be likely to get?

_____

# 4. Prefixes *en-*, *em-*

**The prefixes *en-* and *em-* mean "to cause to be in" or "to provide with something." Sometimes the prefixes are added to base words, as in *enable* and *encircle*, and sometimes they are added to roots that are not complete words, as in *environment*.**

*Read each word and its definition. Then use the word in a sentence.*

1. **employer**: a person or company that hires people to do jobs

   _____

2. **enact**: to pass a law

   _____

3. **enforce**: to make sure people follow a rule or a law

   _____

> The prefix *en-* is more common than *em-*. The prefix *em-* is added to words that start with the letters *b*, *m*, and *p*. For example, *empower*, *embody*.

*Use a word from the list to complete each sentence. Check a dictionary if you don't know the meaning of a word.*

| emphasizes | endanger | enroll |
|---|---|---|

4. Pam will _____ in a safety training class.

5. The company values safety, so it _____ safe behavior in the factory.

6. One careless worker can _____ many people, so everyone must be careful.

# 5. Suffix *-y*

**The suffix *-y* can mean "characterized by." For example, the word *funny* can mean "characterized by fun." Many words that end in *-y* are adjectives that are formed from nouns.**

*Use a word from the list to complete each sentence. Check a dictionary if you don't know the meaning of a word.*

| greasy | noisy | sleepy | slippery | smoky |
|---|---|---|---|---|

1. Rafael slept for only five hours last night. Today he is very _____.

2. When the fire started, the building became very _____. It was hard to see.

3. Someone spilled water on the kitchen floor, so now it is very _____.

4. The machines are loud when they are running, and the shop gets _____.

5. The stove got _____ from fried foods; then a fire started in the kitchen.

> To figure out the meanings of words that have affixes (prefixes or suffixes), look for a familiar word or word part within the word. For example, in the word *sunny*, you can see the word *sun*. This helps you figure out that *sunny* means "characterized by or having light from the sun."

# 6. Compound Words

**If you don't know one of the words in a compound, look up the unfamiliar word. For example, in the compound *fire extinguisher*, you probably know what *fire* means, but you may not know *extinguisher*. If you look it up, you will find that an *extinguisher* is a "metal container with chemicals used for putting out fires."**

*Match each compound word to its definition. Write the correct letter. Use a dictionary if you are unsure of the meaning of a word.*

_____ 1. hard hat

_____ 2. emergency exit

_____ 3. first aid kit

_____ 4. workers' compensation

_____ 5. fire alarm

_____ 6. shirtsleeves

a. insurance that pays workers if they are hurt at work

b. a type of hat worn by building workers to keep their heads safe

c. the sleeves of a shirt

d. a bell or other warning sound that tells people there's a fire

e. a way out of a building or plane during an emergency like a fire

f. a box with materials for treating people with injuries

# 7. Context Clues: General Clues

**When you are trying to figure out the meaning of a word, look for restatements. A restatement says the same thing or presents the same concept in slightly different words.**

Clue words like *this means, that is, also called,* and *in other words* can signal that the writer is restating an idea. A writer may also use punctuation like commas and dashes when restating something.

*Read each sentence. Underline clues that help you understand the boldfaced word. Then write the definition of the word.*

1. Many workplace accidents are **preventable**. One way to stop accidents from happening is to give workers frequent training on safety.

   *Preventable* means _____

2. **Flammable** materials, things that burn easily, should be kept away from sources of heat.

   *Flammable* means _____

3. The employees had to practice **evacuating** the building. In other words, they had to leave and go outside.

   To *evacuate* means _____

4. Workers must take **precautions** when cleaning machines. They can take steps to stop something dangerous from happening by unplugging the machines.

   *Precautions* are _____

5. Elena wears gloves to **protect** her hands. Gloves stop the cleaning chemicals from hurting her skin.

   *Protect* means _____

# 8. Parts of Speech and the Dictionary

**Many words can be used either as nouns or as verbs. A noun names a person, place, thing, or idea. A verb describes an action. Thinking about the part of speech can help you understand a word's meaning.**

*Look up each boldfaced word in a dictionary. Write the part of speech and the definition that matches how the word is used in the sentence.*

1. Clean up **spills** right away so that people don't slip and fall.

   _____ _____

2. Don't leave wires or cords on the floor because people can **trip** over them.

   _____ _____

3. A hard hat can protect your head from **objects** that fall from above.

   _____ _____

4. Workers should **dress** appropriately for the workplace. They should not wear unsafe clothing.

   _____ _____

5. Employees who are tired have a greater **risk** of injury at work.

   _____ _____

● If the word *a*, *an*, or *the* comes right before a word, the word is not a verb. For example, *report* is a noun in this sentence: *You should make a report about the injury.*

● When *object* is a noun, you stress the first syllable: OB-ject. When *object* is a verb, you stress the second syllable: ob-JECT.

# 9. Multiple-Meaning Words

**Some words can have very different meanings Think about the topic you are reading about. Some of the word's possible meanings will not make sense in the context of the sentence.**

*Look at each underlined word. Circle the letter of the best definition.*

1. There were no <u>serious</u> injuries at the factory last year.
   a. quiet and sensible
   b. very bad or dangerous

2. Wear the <u>proper</u> safety gear for your job.
   a. socially acceptable
   b. right or correct

3. You must be careful around machines with moving <u>parts</u>. You can be injured if your clothing or hair gets caught in them.
   a. roles played by actors
   b. a section or piece of something

4. We do a safety <u>drill</u> once a month so that everyone knows how to safely leave the building.
   a. practice for an emergency
   b. a tool for making holes

5. Do not leave food scraps in sinks or on cutting <u>surfaces</u>. It is a health and safety issue.
   a. the flat area used for cooking or working on
   b. the top layer of a body of water

Complete the safety plan with words from the box.

| | | | | | |
|---|---|---|---|---|---|
| accidents | avoidable | dress | emphasize | hard hats | machines |
| objects | precautions | prevent | proper | protect | safety |
| shirtsleeves | slippery | spill | surfaces | trip | |

# Factory Safety Plan

We want to make all areas of our factory safer. We will be sending all employees to

(1) _____ training to learn about ways to (2) _____ injuries.

Below are a few areas that the company wants to

(3) _____, or place importance on.

- Many (4) _____ occur when people use heavy

   equipment and (5) _____. People who work with

   machines must take (6) _____ when handling them.

   For example, if you are cleaning a machine, make sure you unplug it first.

- Everyone in the factory must (7) _____ in appropriate clothing at work. Your

   clothing should make sense for the job you do. For example, if you work around machines, you should

   not have loose (8) _____ or other loose clothing, loose long hair, or jewelry. These

   are (9) _____ that can get caught in moving parts of the machines. Also wear the

   (10) _____ shoes for your job. High-heeled shoes and sandals are not safe here.

- Keep your work area and any work (11) _____ clean. If you

   (12) _____ a liquid, clean it up right away. Water or other liquids can make

   the floor (13) _____. If you drop something, pick it up. Don't let it stay on

   the floor. People might (14) _____ and fall down if they don't see it.

- Wear the right safety gear for your job. All workers in the warehouse must wear

   (15) _____. These keep heads safe if something falls from above. And any

   worker who uses chemicals should wear gloves to (16) _____ the hands.

We believe that most accidents are (17) _____. We hope you will help us create a

safe workplace!

*Read each question. Then circle the best answer.*

1. **Which definition of *serious* matches how the word is used in this passage?**

   If there is a <u>serious</u> injury at work, don't wait. Call 911 immediately.

   **A** very bad or dangerous
   **B** important and needing thought
   **C** quiet and not silly
   **D** worried or unhappy

2. **Which of the following is an example of safety *gear*?**

   **A** shirtsleeves
   **B** an emergency exit
   **C** a hazard
   **D** a hard hat

3. **Which choice best completes the sentence?**

   A fire alarm can _____ you that smoke or flames are in the building.

   **A** harm
   **B** endanger
   **C** ignore
   **D** warn

4. **Which meaning of *parts* matches how the word is used in this sentence?**

   Safety gear can protect different body <u>parts</u>, such as head, hands, and feet.

   **A** pieces of a machine
   **B** lines on a person's head where the hair is combed
   **C** separate areas of a human body
   **D** roles played by actors in a film or play

5. **Which word from the passage means about the same as *preventable*?**

   No one plans to be injured at work. Most job injuries are <u>preventable</u>. One example is injury from repetitive motion, or doing the same thing over and over. Typing, using a computer, and sitting for a long time can injure the arms, back, and eyes. These injuries are avoidable if you stretch and take breaks. Special equipment is also available to reduce these injuries.

   **A** injured
   **B** repetitive
   **C** avoidable
   **D** available

6. **Which word means "to force someone to follow a rule or law"?**

   **A** forceful
   **B** workforce
   **C** enforce
   **D** unenforceable

7. **Which of the following is an example of an *injury*?**

   **A** a room filled with smoke
   **B** a broken leg
   **C** an object falling from above
   **D** a slippery floor

8. **Which choice best completes the passage?**

   After the fire started, the third floor became _____. It was hard to see the exits.

   **A** greasy
   **B** smoky
   **C** chilly
   **D** safety

*Describe how you can be safe at your current job or at a job you know about. Write your answer on a separate sheet of paper. Use at least six words you learned in this unit. Circle the vocabulary words you use.*

*Check your answers on page 108.*

# 12 Losing a Job

## VOCABULARY

Read these words from the passage. Check the words you know.

- [ ] budget
- [ ] compensation
- [ ] debt
- [ ] eligible
- [ ] embarrassed
- [ ] fired
- [ ] former
- [ ] laid off
- [ ] minimum
- [ ] security
- [ ] severance
- [ ] unemployment

### Abbreviation

COBRA (The Consolidated Omnibus Budget Reconciliation Act)

**Anyone can lose a job. It can happen even if you've done nothing wrong. Losing a job is one of the most difficult life experiences that you can go through, even if you didn't much like the job. What should you do if you're fired or laid off?**

Your job is more than just how you make money; it is part of your identity. It gives you a feeling of **security**. Taking charge of your life after you lose your job will help you get that feeling back.

You have rights when you are **fired** or **laid off**. They include the right to any **compensation** you've earned. They may also include **severance**, unused vacation time, and continued healthcare coverage. Ask about your pension and 401(k).

Contact your state **unemployment** office right away and find out if you are **eligible** for unemployment compensation. Most states require you to have worked a **minimum** amount of time in order to collect government benefits. Find out if you meet that requirement. Your unemployment benefit will definitely be less than your salary was, but it will certainly help. Don't be **embarrassed** to claim it.

Continue your health insurance. If you had a health insurance plan with your **former** employer, find out how to pay for one on your own. You may want to apply for COBRA (employer-based health insurance), or you can look into getting your own health insurance. If you're married, see if you can be covered under your spouse's plan.

Look carefully at your monthly expenses and determine which you can cut or reduce. Try not to use up your savings or increase your **debt**. Build a **budget** that cuts down on the amount of money you spend.

Losing your job is one of the most stressful things that can happen to you. Face your feelings and take care of yourself. Talk to your friends and family for support. You can't change what happened, but you can learn from the experience.

*Do you know any other words about unemployment? Write them here.*

_____  _____  _____

# 1. Vocabulary Focus

*Write each word from the list beside its definition.*

| budget | compensation | debt | eligible | embarrassed | fire |
| former | lay off | minimum | security | severance | unemployed |

● The *b* in *debt* is silent. It's pronounced /det/.

● The word *embarrassed* is spelled with *rr* and *ss*.

_____ 1. to let an employee go because his work is unsatisfactory

_____ 2. the smallest number or amount possible

_____ 3. without a job; jobless

_____ 4. having the right to do or get something

_____ 5. payment and other benefits given for doing a job

_____ 6. to let an employee go because the company doesn't have enough work or is reorganizing

_____ 7. feeling uncomfortable and ashamed around other people

_____ 8. extra money and other benefits given to employees who have been laid off

_____ 9. the state of being protected and safe

_____ 10. a plan for how to pay for things

_____ 11. money you owe

_____ 12. from the past; previous

# 2. Use the Vocabulary

*Choose three of the vocabulary words. Define them in your own words.*

1. _____

2. _____

3. _____

*Share your definitions with a partner. Talk about them, and make suggestions for revising them. Rewrite your definitions and share them with the class.*

# 3. Work With New Vocabulary

*Answer the questions. Then compare answers with a partner.*

1. Do you think all employees laid off by one company should receive the same **severance**? Why or why not?

   _____

2. Why is it a good idea to build and follow a **budget**?

   _____

3. Other than money, what kind of **compensation** would you like to receive at work? Why did you choose that option?

   _____

4. What are three reasons a manager might **fire** an employee?

   _____

5. Name two of your **former** teachers whose classes you enjoyed. Explain your choices.

   _____

6. Describe a time when you felt **embarrassed**. What happened?

   _____

7. What are two things you and your family have done to create a sense of **security** in your life and home?

   _____

8. Go online or to the library to find out the **minimum** hourly wage in the state where you live. Do you think that's enough money to live on? Explain your answer.

   _____

9. How do people end up in **debt**? What can they do to get out of debt?

   _____

10. What do you think is the worst thing about being **unemployed**? Why?

    _____

11. Doug was told that he has to **lay off** eight of the people he supervises. What advice would you give Doug for talking to his team?

    _____

12. If you quit your job, do you think you should be **eligible** for unemployment benefits? Why or why not?

    _____

# 4. Prefix un–

The prefix –un means "not" or "opposite of." It creates an antonym, a word that is opposite in meaning to the base word. For example, an unemployed person is not employed, the opposite of being employed.

*Complete each sentence with a word from the list.*

| unable | unexpected | unfair | unnecessary | unprofessional | unused |
|--------|-----------|--------|-------------|----------------|--------|

1. Wayne doesn't have a car, so he is _____ to get to the unemployment office. He's going to apply for his benefits online.

2. Naki got a new job only three days after she was laid off, so it was _____ for her to collect unemployment.

3. When I was fired from the coffee shop, I got paid for all my _____ sick days and vacation days.

4. Don't do anything _____ if you are let go. Watch what you say and do.

5. Sara thought it was _____ that she couldn't collect unemployment benefits right away, but there is a waiting period of one week in New York State.

6. It was completely _____ when five people in tech support were let go. We were all surprised.

> When you add the prefix un– to a word that begins with n, the word is spelled with nn. For example un– + needed is unneeded.

# 5. Suffix –ly

The suffix –ly means "characteristic of" or "in a way that is." When –ly is added to a word, the new word formed is an adverb. For example, the adjective *definite* + the suffix –ly = the adverb *definitely*, which means "in a way that is definite."

friend ➡ friendly    man ➡ manly    mother ➡ motherly    month ➡ monthly

*Rewrite each word below. Add –ly.*

1. financial _____

2. illegal _____

3. professional _____

4. sudden _____

> When you add the suffix –ly to a word that ends with l, the word is spelled with ll. For example personal + –ly is personally.

*Check your answers above. Then use the words to complete the sentences below. Check a dictionary if you don't know the meaning of a word.*

5. You can lose your job _____. Sometimes it happens unexpectedly.

6. Keeping to a budget will make it easier to stay _____ healthy.

7. Experts believe that 200,000 or more workers are _____, or unfairly, fired each year.

8. Try not to say anything negative about your former employer or supervisor. Think and speak _____. Harsh words could hurt you later.

> When the suffix –ly is added to a noun, the new word formed is an adjective.

# 6. Compound Words

**Some phrasal verbs function as compound nouns when they are written as one word. For example,** *cut back* **(two words) is a phrasal verb, but written as** *cutback* **(a closed compound), it's a noun.**

*Complete each sentence with a compound word from the list.*

Nobody knows why a pink slip is called "a pink slip," but everyone knows what it means.

| cutbacks | exit interview | layoff | pink slips | severance package |
| --- | --- | --- | --- | --- |

1. In some states, the employer has to tell you if you lost your job because of a

   _____ or some other general reasons.

2. People who say they got _____ mean that they lost their jobs.

3. Harlan's _____ included continuation of his health care, one month's
   additional salary, and payment for his unused sick and vacation time.

4. Your employer may ask you to do an _____ before you leave the
   company, but you don't have to speak to anyone if you don't want to. Just say, *No thank you.*

5. When there were _____ at the hospital, Fran was worried that she
   would lose her job.

# 7. Context Clues: Examples and General Clues

When you come across a new word, look for clues in the words that come before and after it.

**Sometimes a word's meaning is explained immediately after its use. Look for an explanation or definition inside commas or brackets that follow the word.**

*Read each sentence. Look for clues to the meaning of the boldfaced word. Write the meaning of the word on the line.*

1. If you are let go from your job, you should collect any severance to which you are **entitled**. It
   is your money and you deserve it.

   To be *entitled* means _____

2. Some employers **escort** (walk with) people out of the building when they have been fired.

   To *escort* means _____

3. You can lose your job even when it's not your **fault**. You may not be responsible for a bad
   situation, like a problem with the economy, but you may still get fired or laid off.

   *Fault* means _____

4. Getting fired was difficult, but Dawn is doing her best to **cope**. She is dealing with her
   problems and trying to come up with solutions.

   To *cope* means _____

5. If another company buys and **merges**, or combines, with your company, it's very possible that
   there will be layoffs.

   To *merge* means _____

# 8. Parts of Speech and the Dictionary

**The part of speech identifies how a word is used in a sentence.**

*Look up each boldfaced word in a dictionary. Write the part of speech and the definition that matches how the word is used in the sentence.*

1. Syd asked for a **copy** of all the papers he signed on his last day of work.

   _____  _____

2. If you're fired, don't **blame** your manager or coworkers for your problems at work.

   _____  _____

3. Some states let you file an unemployment **claim** by telephone or online.

   _____  _____

4. Margaret decided to **resign** rather than be fired.

   _____  _____

5. The **stress** of losing her job kept Kelsey up late at night. She couldn't sleep because she was so worried.

   _____  _____

6. When you collect unemployment, you have to report all your **wages** every week.

   _____  _____

● If you know what part of speech a word plays, it's easier to find the correct definition in a dictionary.

● If you see the word *filé* (with an accent mark), it is a seasoning used in cooking.

# 9. Multiple-Meaning Words

**Many words have two or more meanings even though they may be spelled and pronounced the same way.**

*Look at the underlined word in each sentence. Circle the letter of the best definition.*

1. You can <u>elect</u> to continue your health insurance through COBRA or you can buy an individual plan.
   a. to vote for someone for a position, job, etc.
   b. to choose to do something

2. If you lose your job, look for ways to <u>reduce</u> your spending.
   a. to make something smaller
   b. to lose weight

3. Ms. Ingram explained the company <u>policy</u> on training, expectations, and benefits.
   a. a written agreement with an insurance company
   b. an accepted set of rules for how to do something

4. Kenny was escorted out of the store by <u>security</u>.
   a. the state of being safe
   b. the guards who protect a business

*Complete the poster. Use words from the list.*

| claim | compensation | entitled | fault | unemployment | weekly |
|---|---|---|---|---|---|

## LOST YOUR JOB? WHAT'S NEXT?

If you have lost your job through no (1) _____

of your own and worked a certain number of hours, you

may be (2) _____ to government benefits.

You just need to file your (3) _____ with the

(4) _____ office in the state where you worked.

Your benefits won't match your salary, but

the (5) _____ checks will help

pay your monthly bills. So take the money. It's

(6) _____ that you've earned.

## @lostyourjob

*Complete the paragraph. Use words from the list.*

| embarrassed | escort | fired | pink slip | policy | security | stress | unnecessary |
|---|---|---|---|---|---|---|---|

When Arley was (7) _____ from his job, he was asked to leave the building immediately.

Someone from (8) _____ walked him to his car. Although he knew it was company

(9) _____, Arley thought it was (10) _____ for him to have an

(11) _____. He felt a little (12) _____.

Arley did his best to keep it all together until he got home. He knew that his friends and family would help him

deal with the (13) _____ of getting a (14) _____.

*Read each question. Then circle the best answer.*

1. **What does the word *fire* mean in this question?**

   Under federal law, your employer doesn't have to give a reason to <u>fire</u> you.

   **A** to shoot a gun

   **B** to let someone go from a job

   **C** to give energy to

   **D** to throw something fast and hard

2. **Which definition of *files* matches how the word is used in this sentence?**

   Michael took home a box of his personal items and <u>files</u> from his desk before he resigned.

   **A** lines of people or things one behind another

   **B** folders for keeping papers in order

   **C** metal tools with a rough surface used to smooth things

   **D** collections of data on a computer

3. **Complete the sentence.**

   Even though he thought it wasn't his _____, Jerry was fired when the machine broke down.

   **A** fault

   **B** blame

   **C** stress

   **D** policy

4. **Which word or words from the passage mean about the same as *eligible for*?**

   Ariel was <u>eligible for</u> unemployment benefits after she lost her job. She knew she was entitled to severance. Because she was laid off, she also claimed unused vacation days.

   **A** lost

   **B** claimed

   **C** laid off

   **D** entitled to

5. **Which word best completes the sentence?**

   Blair was very surprised when he was let go. He had no idea the firm was cutting back. It was totally _____.

   **A** unexpected

   **B** unprofessional

   **C** unemployed

   **D** unnecessary

6. **Which of the following words means "the smallest amount of something"?**

   **A** cutback

   **B** unfair

   **C** minimum

   **D** budget

7. **Which choice best completes the sentence?**

   Franklin wanted to be sure he wasn't fired _____, so he talked to a counselor at the unemployment office.

   **A** suddenly

   **B** professionally

   **C** financially

   **D** illegally

8. **What does the word *copy* mean in this sentence?**

   When Talisa was fired, she asked to <u>copy</u> all of the papers that she had to sign.

   **A** to make an identical version of; duplicate

   **B** to take someone else's ideas and use them

   **C** to send someone a copy of an email message

   **D** to do something in the same way as someone else

*Imagine that your best friend has just been laid off. Give him or her your best advice about what to do and what to expect. Write your answer on a separate sheet of paper. Use at least six words you learned in this unit. Circle the vocabulary words you use.*

*Check your answers on page 108.*

# Answer Key

## UNIT 1

### Exercise 1, p. 9
1. job fair
2. training
3. keyword
4. network
5. benefits
6. hire
7. employment
8. salary
9. temporary
10. apply
11. skills
12. employer

### Exercise 4, p. 11
1. deposit
2. compose
3. posture
4. post
5. position
6. proposal

### Exercise 5, p. 11
1. hopeful
2. successful
3. stressful
4. careful
5. thoughtful; sentences will vary.
6. helpful; sentences will vary.

### Exercise 6, p. 12
1. workforce
2. workweek
3. full-time
4. part-time
5. job board

### Exercise 7, p. 12
1. looking for
2. to make
3. chance
4. job
5. pay
6. gives

### Exercise 8, p. 13
Definitions will vary.
1. noun
2. verb
3. verb
4. adjective
5. noun

### Exercise 9, p. 13
1. b          4. a
2. b          5. b
3. a

### Review, p. 14
1. successful
2. job fair
3. plan
4. hunt
5. workforce
6. hopeful
7. stressful
8. provide
9. seeking
10. skills
11. match
12. training
13. apply
14. job board
15. employers

### Review, p. 15
1. B          5. D
2. A          6. A
3. D          7. C
4. B          8. C

## UNIT 2

### Exercise 1, p. 17
1. j          7. a
2. i          8. l
3. f          9. c
4. e          10. k
5. g          11. d
6. h          12. b

### Exercise 4, p. 19
1.–3. Sentences will vary.
4. return
5. reread
6. recall

### Exercise 5, p. 19
1. position
2. qualifications
3. application
4. discussion

### Exercise 6, p. 20
1. workforce center
2. websites
3. double check
4. feedback
5. guidelines

### Exercise 7, p. 20
Definitions will vary.

### Exercise 8, p. 21
Definitions will vary.
1. verb
2. verb
3. verb
4. verb
5. noun

### Exercise 9, p. 21
1. a          4. a
2. b          5. a
3. b

### Review, p. 22
1. steps
2. guidelines
3. sample
4. references
5. contact information
6. accurate
7. chronological
8. legibly
9. screen
10. blanks
11. applicable
12. submit
13. proofread

### Review, p. 23
1. B          5. B
2. D          6. D
3. C          7. A
4. B          8. A

## UNIT 3

### Exercise 1, p. 25
1. g          7. e
2. i          8. l
3. h          9. a
4. b          10. k
5. j          11. f
6. c          12. d

### Exercise 4, p. 27
1. impression
2. include
3. improve
4. increases

**Exercise 5, p. 27**

Definitions will vary.

**Exercise 6, p. 28**

1. showcase
2. summary statement
3. job opening
4. people skills
5. spell-check
6. brainstorm

**Exercise 7, p. 28**

Definitions will vary.

**Exercise 8, p. 29**

1. noun
2. verb
3. noun
4. verb
5. noun
6. verb

**Exercise 9, p. 29**

1. b
2. a
3. a
4. b
5. b

**Review, p. 30**

1. research
2. job opening
3. summary statement
4. accomplishment
5. emphasized
6. keywords
7. team player
8. spell-check
9. cover letter
10. brainstorm
11. specific
12. include
13. documents
14. informative

**Review, p. 31**

1. B
2. A
3. C
4. A
5. D
6. B
7. D
8. D

## UNIT 4

**Exercise 1, p. 33**

1. offer
2. prepare
3. candidate
4. decision
5. impression
6. common
7. screen
8. appropriately
9. contribute
10. valuable
11. interview
12. convince

**Exercise 4, p. 35**

Answers will vary.

**Exercise 5, p. 35**

1. transcribe
2. describe
3. subscription
4. transcript
5. script

**Exercise 6, p. 36**

1. handshake
2. eye contact
3. business card
4. hiring manager
5. job description

**Exercise 7, p. 36**

Answers may vary.

1. asked him questions, helped him improve answers
2. pants, a long-sleeved shirt, and a tie

3. math skills, people skills, and customer service experience
4. cell phones, chargers, and cases
5. greeting customers, talking about the products, and making sales

**Exercise 8, p. 37**

Definitions will vary.

1. noun
2. verb
3. verb
4. noun
5. noun

**Exercise 9, p. 37**

1. b
2. a
3. b
4. b
5. a

**Review, p. 38**

1. screen
2. interview
3. positive
4. impression
5. prepare
6. Internet
7. common
8. answer
9. hiring manager
10. describe
11. job description
12. requirements
13. convince
14. contribute
15. interrupt
16. appropriately
17. attire

**Review, p. 39**

1. D
2. A
3. C
4. A
5. B
6. D
7. C
8. D

## UNIT 5

**Exercise 1, p. 41**

1. integrity
2. reliable
3. hobby
4. professional
5. policies
6. dress code
7. lack
8. expectation
9. diverse
10. attitude
11. honest
12. fundamental

**Exercise 4, p. 43**

1. disagree
2. dishonest
3. disability
4. disrespect
5. distrust

**Exercise 5, p. 43**

1. employability
2. equality
3. responsibility
4. difficulty
5. honesty
6. possibility

**Exercise 6, p. 44**

1. e
2. d
3. f
4. a
5. c
6. b

**Exercise 7, p. 44**

Definitions will vary.

**Exercise 8, p. 45**

1. verb
2. noun
3. verb
4. verb
5. noun
6. verb

**Exercise 9, p. 45**
1. b     4. a
2. b     5. a
3. a

**Review, p. 46**
1. Professional
2. attitude
3. diverse
4. expectations
5. spotlight
6. Report
7. team player
8. count
9. responsibilities
10. exceeds
11. honest
12. manage

**Review, p. 47**
1. A     5. A
2. B     6. C
3. A     7. A
4. B     8. D

**UNIT 6**

**Exercise 1, p. 49**
1. motivate
2. collaborate
3. role
4. flexible
5. volunteer
6. dispute
7. teamwork
8. responsibility
9. divide
10. effective
11. individual
12. opinion

**Exercise 4, p. 51**
1. colleagues
2. communicate
3. collect
4. confirmed
5. conference

6. compromise

**Exercise 5, p. 51**
Definitions will vary.

**Exercise 6, p. 52**
1. deadline
2. newsletter
3. conference room
4. team leader
5. problem-solving

**Exercise 7, p. 52**
1. very important
2. person in charge
3. give someone a task
4. jobs
5. work well together
6. rely

**Exercise 8, p. 53**
Definitions will vary.
1. adjective
2. noun
3. verb
4. verb
5. noun

**Exercise 9, p. 53**
1. b     4. b
2. a     5. a
3. b

**Review, p. 54**
1. assigned
2. project
3. divide
4. deadline
5. role
6. individual
7. teamwork
8. manager
9. responsible
10. delegates
11. tasks
12. volunteer
13. goals
14. opinions

15. dispute
16. communicate
17. flexible

**Review, p. 55**
1. D     5. C
2. C     6. B
3. A     7. B
4. A     8. C

**UNIT 7**

**Exercise 1, p. 57**
1. focus
2. commitment
3. measure
4. define
5. accountable
6. realistic
7. challenging
8. progress
9. obstacle
10. method
11. vary
12. achieve

**Exercise 4, p. 59**
Definitions will vary.

**Exercise 5, p. 59**
1. willingness
2. preparedness
3. greatness
4. awareness
5. correctness

**Exercise 6, p. 60**
1. short-term
2. workplace
3. roadblock
4. time frame
5. long-term
6. milestone

**Exercise 7, p. 60**
Definitions will vary.

**Exercise 8, p. 61**
Definitions will vary.

1. verb
2. verb
3. adjective
4. verb
5. noun

**Exercise 9, p. 61**
1. a     4. a
2. b     5. b
3. a

**Review, p. 62**
1. complete
2. achieve
3. long-term
4. impossible
5. willingness
6. posted
7. awareness
8. method
9. define
10. general
11. measure
12. progress
13. share
14. accountable
15. obstacles
16. face

**Review, p. 63**
1. D     5. C
2. C     6. A
3. C     7. A
4. A     8. B

**UNIT 8**

**Exercise 1, p. 65**
1. supervisor
2. compare
3. objective
4. critical
5. performance appraisal
6. evaluate
7. promotion
8. probation

9. improve
10. defensive
11. performance
12. monitor

**Exercise 4, p. 67**

Definitions will vary.

**Exercise 5, p. 67**

1. b      4. e
2. f      5. c
3. a      6. d
7. Sentences will vary.

**Exercise 6, p. 68**

1. workload
2. human resources
3. action plan
4. one-sided
5. point of view
6. highlight

**Exercise 7, p. 68**

Definitions will vary.

**Exercise 8, p. 69**

Definitions will vary.

1. adjective
2. noun
3. verb
4. verb
5. adjective

**Exercise 9, p. 69**

1. a      4. a
2. b      5. a
3. b

**Review, p. 70**

1. overworked
2. handle
3. discuss
4. supervisor
5. oversees
6. workload
7. critical
8. point of view

9. valid
10. human resources
11. probation
12. trial
13. period
14. monitors
15. objectives
16. evaluates
17. regular

**Review, p. 71**

1. C      5. D
2. B      6. B
3. C      7. B
4. A      8. D

## UNIT 9

**Exercise 1, p. 73**

1. match
2. retirement
3. insurance
4. disability
5. Social Security
6. enroll
7. vested
8. contribute
9. personal days
10. accrue
11. qualify
12. matters

**Exercise 4, p. 75**

1. bonus
2. beneficial
3. bounty
4. benefit
5. beneficiary

**Exercise 5, p. 75**

1. payment
2. investment
3. advertisement
4. reimbursement
5. replacement

**Exercise 6, p. 76**

1. stock options
2. flexible spending account
3. income tax
4. childcare
5. flextime
6. open enrollment

**Exercise 7, p. 76**

1. guarantee
2. premium
3. comprehensive
4. dependents
5. welfare

**Exercise 8, p. 77**

Definitions will vary.

**Exercise 9, p. 77**

1. a      4. b
2. a      5. a
3. b

**Review, p. 78**

1. open enrollment
2. firm
3. insurance
4. vested
5. contribute
6. match
7. flexible spending account
8. childcare
9. qualify
10. costs
11. personal days
12. value

**Review, p. 79**

1. D      5. B
2. A      6. B
3. C      7. C
4. A      8. B

## UNIT 10

**Exercise 1, p. 81**

1. h      7. b
2. l      8. c
3. j      9. g
4. f      10. i
5. a      11. d
6. e      12. k

**Exercise 4, p. 83**

Definitions will vary.

**Exercise 5, p. 83**

1. optional
2. dental
3. personal
4. financial
5. original
6. additional
7. national
8. commercial

**Exercise 6, p. 84**

1. taxable income
2. pay rate
3. income tax
4. overtime pay
5. payroll
6. bonus pay

**Exercise 7, p. 84**

1. yearly
2. can't exchange for money
3. mixed and different
4. influence
5. determined mathematically
6. get advice from

**Exercise 8, p. 85**

1. verb
2. verb
3. verb
4. verb

5. noun
Definitions will vary.

**Exercise 9, page 85**
1. b        4. b
2. a        5. b
3. b

**Review, p. 86**
1. annual
2. pay period
3. gross pay
4. deductions
5. dental
6. income taxes
7. paycheck
8. net pay
9. payroll
10. access
11. account
12. financial
13. dependents
14. federal
15. withholds

**Review, p. 87**
1. B        5. B
2. A        6. C
3. A        7. B
4. D        8. D

## UNIT 11

**Exercise 1, p. 89**
1. avoidable
2. gear
3. injury
4. harm
5. hazard
6. machine
7. Safety
8. accident
9. warn
10. ignore
11. prevent
12. dangerous

**Exercise 4, p. 91**
1.–3. Sentences will vary.
4. enroll
5. emphasizes
6. endanger

**Exercise 5, p. 91**
1. sleepy
2. smoky
3. slippery
4. noisy
5. greasy

**Exercise 6, p. 92**
1. b        4. a
2. e        5. d
3. f        6. c

**Exercise 7, p. 92**
Definitions will vary.

**Exercise 8, p. 93**
Definitions will vary.
1. noun
2. verb
3. noun
4. verb
5. noun

**Exercise 9, p. 93**
1. b        4. a
2. b        5. a
3. b

**Review, p. 94**
1. safety
2. prevent
3. emphasize
4. accidents
5. machines
6. precautions
7. dress
8. shirtsleeves
9. objects
10. proper
11. surfaces
12. spill

13. slippery
14. trip
15. hard hats
16. protect
17. avoidable

**Review. p. 95**
1. A        5. C
2. D        6. C
3. D        7. B
4. C        8. B

## UNIT 12

**Exercise 1, p. 97**
1. fire
2. minimum
3. unemployed
4. eligible
5. compensation
6. lay off
7. embarrassed
8. severance
9. security
10. budget
11. debt
12. former

**Exercise 4, p. 99**
1. unable
2. unnecessary
3. unused
4. unprofessional
5. unfair
6. unexpected

**Exercise 5, p. 99**
1. financially
2. illegally
3. professionally
4. suddenly
5. suddenly
6. financially
7. illegally
8. professionally

**Exercise 6, p. 100**
1. layoff
2. pink slips
3. severance package
4. exit interview
5. cutbacks

**Exercise 7, p. 100**
Answers will vary.

**Exercise 8, p. 101**
Definitions will vary.
1. noun
2. verb
3. noun
4. verb
5. noun
6. noun

**Exercise 9, p. 101**
1. b        3. b
2. a        4. b

**Review, p. 102**
1. fault
2. entitled
3. claim
4. unemployment
5. weekly
6. compensation
7. fired
8. security
9. policy
10. unnecessary
11. escort
12. embarrassed
13. stress
14. pink slip

**Review, p. 103**
1. B        5. A
2. B        6. C
3. A        7. D
4. D        8. A

# Appendix I: Common Prefixes

| Prefix | Meaning | Example |
|---|---|---|
| anti– | against | antibiotic |
| **col–** **com–** **con–** | with, together | collect communicate confirm |
| de– | opposite, down | decrease |
| **dis–** | not, opposite of | disagree |
| **em–** **en–** | cause to | employer endanger |
| fore– | before | foresee |
| **il–** **in–** **im–** **ir–** | not, opposite of | illegal indirect impossible irresponsible |
| **in–** **im–** | in or into | invite immigrate |
| **inter–** | among, between | interact |
| mid– | middle | midterm |
| mis– | wrongly | misspeak |
| multi– | many | multiple |
| non– | not, opposite of | nonsense |
| **over–** | too much, above | overreact |
| **pre–** | before | presell |
| **re–** | again, back | restart |
| semi– | half | semicircle |
| sub– | under, lower | subtitle |
| super– | above, beyond | supermarket |
| **un–** | not, opposite of | unhappy |
| under– | too little, below | underrated underground |

Prefixes in **boldface** are taught in this book.

# Appendix II: Common Suffixes

| Suffix | Meaning | Example |
|---|---|---|
| **-able**<br>**-ible** | is, can be | available<br>responsible |
| **-al**<br>-ial | having characteristics of | personal<br>financial |
| **-ation**<br>**-cation**<br>**-ion**<br>**-tion** | act, process | organization<br>education<br>occasion<br>definition |
| -ed | past form of verbs | wanted |
| -en | made of | wooden |
| -er | comparative | longer |
| -er<br>-or | one who | teacher<br>inventor |
| -est | superlative | deepest |
| **-ful** | full of | careful |
| -ic | having characteristics of | scientific |
| -ing | present participle | speaking |
| -ist | one who practices | artist |
| **-ity**<br>**-ty** | state of | activity<br>difficulty |
| **-ive**<br>**-ative**<br>**-itive** | adjective form of a noun | decisive<br>informative<br>repetitive |
| -less | without | worthless |
| -logy | study of | biology |
| **-ly** | characteristic of | happily |
| **-ment** | action or process | employment |
| **-ness** | state of, condition of | awareness |
| -ous<br>-eous<br>-ious | possessing the qualities of | dangerous<br>righteous<br>serious |
| -s<br>-es | plural | books<br>boxes |
| **-y** | characterized by | noisy |

Suffixes in **boldface** are taught in this book.

# Appendix III: Common Roots

| Root | Meaning | Example |
|------|---------|---------|
| audi | hear | audience |
| auto | self | automobile |
| **bene** **bon** **boun** | good, well | benefit bonus bountiful |
| bio | life | biology |
| cycle | circle | recycle |
| dic dict | say | dictate predict |
| duc duct | make, lead | produce conduct |
| geo | earth | geography |
| graph | write | paragraph |
| jur jus | law | jury justice |
| mand mend | order | command recommend |
| meter metr | measure | perimeter geometry |
| phon | sound | telephone |
| port | carry | transport |
| **pos** | place | deposit |
| **scrib** **script** | write | scribble prescription |
| tele | far off | television |
| therm | heat | thermometer |
| trans | across | transport |
| **val** | worth, strength, health | evaluate |
| vid vis | see | video vision |

Roots in **boldface** are taught in this book.

# Personal Dictionary

*Create your own dictionary. Write down any words you want to remember.*

| Word | Definition | Used in a Sentence | Notes |
|------|-----------|--------------------|-------|
|      |           |                    |       |
|      |           |                    |       |
|      |           |                    |       |
|      |           |                    |       |
|      |           |                    |       |
|      |           |                    |       |
|      |           |                    |       |
|      |           |                    |       |
|      |           |                    |       |
|      |           |                    |       |
|      |           |                    |       |
|      |           |                    |       |
|      |           |                    |       |
|      |           |                    |       |
|      |           |                    |       |
|      |           |                    |       |
|      |           |                    |       |